STELLA EZE

BACK FROM THE DEAD

A True Account of How God Miraculously Brought My Dead Child Back to Life

Copyright © 2024 Stella Ezekweh

All rights reserved.

ISBN -13: 9798324121082

This book, or parts thereof, may not be reproduced or transmitted in any form or by any means, electronic or mechanical, including recording, photocopying, offset, or by any information storage and retrieval system without permission in writing from the author.

 Zion Publishing

Australia – Barbados – China – India – Japan – New Zealand
South Africa – United Kingdom – United States

Published in the United Kingdom by
Zion Publishing
For information about publishing with Zion Publishing, please contact us on our Facebook: ZionVsolutions (Zion Virtual Outreach)

DEDICATION

This book is dedicated to God the Father, God the Son, and God the Holy Spirit, through whose inspiration, prodding, fortitude, knowledge, and wisdom I was able to complete it.

To my charming and affable daughter who has granted me permission to share her story.

To my wonderful family, who have been incredibly supportive and caring.

To the doctors and medical personnel in Hannover, Germany, whose medical expertise, and professionalism were divinely orchestrated by the Almighty God, for taking such excellent care of my daughter in the hospital.

And, finally, to everyone who will read this book and find something to strengthen their faith.

TABLE OF CONTENTS

DEDICATION iv

ACKNOWLEDGEMENTS vi

FOREWORD vii

PREFACE x

INTRODUCTION xii

CHAPTER 1: LIFE IN THE INTENSIVE CARE UNIT 1

CHAPTER 2: TRUSTING THE GREAT PHYSICIAN 11

CHAPTER 3: HOPE UPON IMPACT 18

CHAPTER 4: AND MY BABY DIED 26

CHAPTER 5: GRATITUDE IN GRIEF 38

CHAPTER 6: GOD OF THE IMPOSSIBLE 47

CHAPTER 7: EL ROI THE GOD WHO SEES ME 59

CHAPTER 8: OUR AFFLICTIONS ARE TRANSIENT 69

CHAPTER 9: BYE HOSPITAL. WELCOME HOME 78

CHAPTER 10: HOSPITAL EVANGELISM IS BORN 95

ABOUT THE AUTHOR 104

ACKNOWLEDGEMENTS

This book was composed under the guidance of the Holy Spirit and based on a personal story. I am confident that you will find it fulfilling because of the consistent display of faith that people respond to whenever I share this testimony. As a result, I trust that *Back From The Dead* will inspire and reinforce more people's faith in Jesus' name.

First and foremost, I am eternally grateful to God the Father, the Son, and the Holy Spirit for helping me complete this book successfully. I am also eternally grateful for the salvation of my soul and the honour of being called a child of God.

My heartfelt thanks go to my amazing and exceptional family. Thank you all for believing in me. May God continue to shine His face upon you all. I adore you all.

Finally, I want to express my heartfelt gratitude to Pastor Gordon Hurd, my Editor and Co-publisher and his family. Thank you very much, sir, for believing in me. God bless you for your encouragement and support.

Stella Ezekweh

FOREWORD

Stella's book *Back From The Dead*, is a true story of the wonders of Jehovah Rapha and a testament to the fact that even today, our God is performing miracles.

As believers, we accept that Jesus healed the Centurion's servant, restored the sight of blind Bartimaeus, took leprosy from Naaman, and healed the woman with the issue of blood. What we usually find hard to believe is the fact that an amputated leg can grow instantly in church, or that a decaying head can be restored without medical intervention.

Today, especially with the advance of, and reliance on, modern medicine, our faith has shifted to the logic of medical science and the consensus seems to be, to our eternal shame, that if the medics cannot do it, then it must be witchcraft if it is done. How many times have we rushed to condemn a Man of God today after he raises a dead person or heals a chronic illness in the Name of Jesus?

Stella's true story is, therefore, a strong reminder to anyone faced with an impossible situation, any situation at all, that we can still draw miraculous healing and restoration from the throne of mercy. The Holy Spirit is still here and ready to perform the impossible if we surrender our situation to Him.

Just over a decade ago, I received a phone call from my wife

BACK FROM THE DEAD

that our son Excellence, aged 3 years at the time, had crawled through the first-floor window of our house in Liverpool and dropped about 10 meters onto a concrete surface. My first thought was how I would support him with the inevitable brain damage that would follow the fall. My second thought though was more radical. On my way to the Alder Hey Children's Hospital to see him, I also declared war. I said to the kingdom of darkness, "You have touched the wrong child. I will draw upon the power of Almighty God and bring down healing upon this child and upon any other sick child I encounter from this day forward".

When I got to his bedside, I was unprepared for what I saw. He screamed "Daddy"! Then he leapt from the bed and hugged me. The nurses told me they did not believe he fell as not only did he not have any external bruises, but the CT scan returned no anomaly. I fell on my face and wept for joy. My son later recounted that when he jumped from the window, someone wearing white clothes caught him and placed him on the concrete gently. His mum, moved by the miraculous saving of our son, began to go on buses to preach the healing power of God.

That is why this book resonates with me. I have experienced, first-hand, God's ability to do the impossible.

So, as you read this book, *Back From The Dead*, I want you

BACK FROM THE DEAD

to draw renewed faith from the restoration of Stella's blessed child to deal with any situation you may be facing right now. If God can raise Stella's child from the dead, what can He not do for you? The Bible says in Hebrews 11:16, that "without faith, it is impossible to please God because anyone who comes to Him must believe that He exists and that He rewards those who earnestly seek Him".

May your faith be renewed as you read this book so that you will live a life of victory over disease, poverty, and all forms of evil until the coming of our Lord and Saviour Jesus Christ.

Gordon Hurd
Life Coach, Provocateur, Publisher, Author, Minister, Philanthropist, Media Strategist, Father, Husband, and Student.
Author of *Christian Prosperity Secrets* (Amazon)
YouTube: @BigManTyrone
Facebook: @mrgordonhurd
Twitter: @BasedTyrone

BACK FROM THE DEAD

PREFACE

Have you ever hesitated to pray because you thought you were making an impossible request? Is your heart plagued by fear or doubt due to an overwhelming challenge?

Perhaps you are not receiving an answer to a longstanding issue, and wondering if you should just quit praying. You are not alone. I also encountered what appeared to be an impossible scenario, but our God emerged and showed me His incredibly great power.

If, like me at the time my daughter died, you are facing a challenge that seems intractable, I want you to find assurance in this book and know that our God is the same yesterday, today and forever.

As the stone at Lazarus' tomb was rolled away in the Bible and Lazarus came alive, God rolled away all the negativity and affliction in the life of my daughter so that she may live. God's gift makes us rich and adds no sorrow. Her case ended in praise, yes, it did.

I carried out some spiritual exercises during my child's ordeal, and they are detailed in this book. I am not asserting that God reacted to these actions, but they are all part of the testimony. It is possible that God extended His mercy in response to these humble demonstrations of faith. Remember Jesus told us that He fasted for forty days; if it were unimportant, he would not have mentioned it. It also prepares us to do the same when required. To gain God's favour in the Old Testament, people donned sackcloth and poured ashes on their heads. In the New Testament, however, people fast to obtain God's mercy or for spiritual growth. We need to acknowledge that God communicates with each of us in a unique manner, but it is also advantageous to learn from the experiences of others.

Join me in praising the God of consolation, miracles, happiness, serenity, fulfilment, and love. Let us worship the majesty of our God that can do all things.

Stella Ezekweh

BACK FROM THE DEAD

INTRODUCTION

The concept of God's healing appears throughout the Bible's sacred pages, carrying significance and bringing hope and redemption to believers throughout history. The Bible is replete with tales of life triumphing over death, from raising the widow of Zarephath's son in 1 Kings 17:17-24 (Old Testament) to raising Dorcas in Acts 9:36-43. These stories showcase the transformative power of God's divine intervention.

In *Back from the Dead*, we learn about God's miraculous power, which attests to the fact of God's intervention with mankind. In this book, we will look at how the Holy Spirit arranged this miraculous event. We will also examine how crucial it is to listen to the Holy Spirit and follow His instructions. The orders that followed resulted in the triumph.

Back from the Dead is a powerful reflection on our work with the Holy Spirit; it inspires us to be consistent and never give up. The most important thing is to strengthen our faith and hold onto God's Word. We are urged to assess our own work with the Holy Spirit, and how frequently we let Him take the lead.

Back from the Dead shows how to handle uncertainties and fears by relying on God's unfailing Word and love. The promise of God brings the ultimate victory and gives us hope in the face of life's greatest challenges. *Back from the Dead* challenges us to accept the great mystery of God's Word and to live fearlessly, confident in the knowledge that we are more than conquerors. This book encourages readers to place more trust in God's Word in their spiritual journey with Christ by examining how God's Word may give new life and hope to everyone who dares to believe.

Dr Ruth Baje
(Author and Pastor)

BACK FROM THE DEAD

"When you pass through the waters, I will be with you; and when you pass through the rivers, they will not sweep over you".
(Isaiah 43:2)

CHAPTER 1

LIFE IN THE INTENSIVE CARE UNIT

The miraculous experience of my daughter dying and coming back to life will live with me forever. God is awesome and He has proved Himself again and again. May His name be praised forever.

While attending antenatal classes, I learned that a full-term pregnancy is one that lasts between 38 and 40 weeks. My pregnancy was over 40 weeks when the worry began, because a pregnancy that lasts longer than 42 weeks is considered post-term by medical professionals. My pregnancy was almost post-term, which means it was prolonged. When a baby is overdue, a membrane sweep may

BACK FROM THE DEAD

be the first thing a person is offered, depending on the practice. The membrane sweep increases the likelihood to go into labour naturally. This was the first option that was presented to me. Every one of my children was unique, demonstrating that every pregnancy and labour is unique. Everything went well in the pregnancy, with the exception of the baby being deemed 'large' two weeks before the due date.

Thankfully, nature finally made her move after my due date, and I went into labour amid all my concerns and anxiety. The cramps came every two to three minutes and grew severe over the following hour. "All right", I reasoned, "it's hospital time".

Contractions had become more intense, and I clenched my teeth and breathed through. The contractions became even harsher while I registered at the hospital and was moved to the labour and delivery ward. Every squeeze in my pelvis hurt deeply and made me curl my toes and groan. In all, I knew God was at work. The nurse encouraged me and assured me it would not be too long.

It did not take long, and my baby arrived, after a brief delay, "Stella, look!" I turned to see a baby, gorgeous, moist, and wiggling and placed in my body in the most intimate way possible. I embraced my baby and said hello. She yelled at

LIFE IN THE INTENSIVE CARE UNIT

my voice, which instantly melted my heart. My baby had already been cleaned, wrapped, and presented to me by the time my husband arrived.

My husband was astounded by how quickly our beautiful baby had arrived and thanked God for her safe delivery. Even though I was mentally and physically exhausted, tears of joy overflowed as I was finally able to hold my newborn baby in my arms. It is advised that a newborn baby be placed skin-to-skin as soon as possible, irrespective of where and how the child is delivered, as long as both mum and child are in good health.

My ordeal began after only 10 minutes of skin-to-skin contact, and we were told that my baby's heartbeat was not functioning correctly. Our mental attitude shifted. My daughter, who was enjoying her mum's hugging, began to experience breathing difficulties, which got increasingly unpleasant as the seconds and minutes passed. Soon after, my husband held an emergency multi-agency meeting with the doctors, followed by a best-interest decision meeting to transport my daughter to a heart and lung specialist hospital, five hours away from her birthplace.

All of this occurred when I was still recovering from delivery. I saw my baby removed from me, and my entire life fell apart I

BACK FROM THE DEAD

could not sleep the entire night because I kept thinking about how delicate she felt in my arms. I was waiting for daybreak so that I might be taken to see her. Without going into detail, the doctors advised that her breathing was extremely difficult. I was miserable and vulnerable, plagued with a variety of thoughts. At that point, I resolved that it had been God all along and that He would not fail me. The next day, an ambulance took me to the hospital where she was hospitalised.

Upon my arrival at the hospital, my baby was already in the ICU with all the stabilisation machines to keep her heart stable. Fear prevented me from approaching her as I stood far away and sobbed uncontrollably. I was stunned by the multitude of devices inserted into her.

Patients in an ICU who are in critical care are continuously monitored by a team of ICU personnel. They are hooked up to equipment via a variety of tubes, cables, and connections. This technology is used to monitor a patient's health and keep their physiological functions intact while they recuperate. Also, anaesthesiologists routinely administer sedatives and painkillers to intensive care unit patients. This is due to the possibility that patients will not be able to handle the discomfort caused by some of the technology currently being used. Even so, my daughter was sedated without eating for three weeks. For us, it was very traumatic.

LIFE IN THE INTENSIVE CARE UNIT

After the initial shock, I gained confidence and moved closer to my child. The love of a mother engulfed my entire being. Although I had the desire to immediately lift her, I was constrained by the restrictions she was surrounded with. I realised I could not hold her as tightly as when she first arrived. In my anxiety, I attempted to convey to the ICU staff that I had previously held and caressed her, but my words went unnoticed as the attending physicians and nurses hurriedly added medication into the infusion. I felt quite vulnerable during that difficult and scary period of my life.

The situation soon became more distressing, and tears flowed down my cheeks. At that time, I realised that God had given me the baby and that His gift is prosperous and adds no sorrow. I was optimistic that it would end in praise, contrary to what the devil had intended.

Later that day, I returned to my hotel room as parents were not permitted to stay in the ward. When I arrived, I prayed to the God of impossibilities saying, "If you have given me this child, no one can steal her from me". I made a vow to skip breakfast until my child returned home. Breakfast may seem like a little, but as a woman who had recently given birth and required additional nutrients to stay healthy, it was vital that I had breakfast and that was my little sacrifice. In addition, I made the decision that until my daughter's case was resolved,

BACK FROM THE DEAD

I would engage in warfare prayers every day at midnight.

I continued to believe in God, and soon after, I heard from God that my daughter's sickness was not meant for her to die, but rather to exalt the name of God. My reliance on God's Word became greater and firmer throughout. I shall never forget the verse John 17:1. Before Jesus was taken up, He said to his father, "Father, glorify your son so that your son may glorify you." I continued hoping that Jesus would glorify Himself through my baby. Whenever the devil tried to deceive me, I went straight to my Bible and read that specific rhema Word. I clutched that Word so closely as if my life depended on it. Every time I read those lines from the Bible, as this was the only hope I had, I felt revitalised and hopeful. I began to ponder and reflect on God's faithfulness.

In the midst of everything that was happening, I learned that the general overseer of the Redeemed Christian Church of God and his lovely wife were visiting our city. I took a photo of my daughter to the event. Though it was a large crowd, I approached the general overseer's wife as soon as I spotted them enter their vehicle. Despite the protocol personnel's attempt to stop me, as soon as the general overseer's wife spotted me, she requested permission for me to see her. I then showed the photograph of my baby to her, she asked where she was. I informed her of her critical condition and her hospital admission. She said it was well with her, and that I would testify. Those words brought me so much succour; it

LIFE IN THE INTENSIVE CARE UNIT

was like the precious ointment that ran down upon the beard, even Aaron's beard that went down to the skirts of his garments (Psalm 133:2) Alleluia!

Despite this, I persisted in the fast and battle at midnight in the event that my baby was ensnared in a coven. The more I persevered, the more it appeared that I was pouring water on a duck's back, as there was no positive report from the doctors, and life seemed so empty without my baby. Then I heard 2 Kings 3:17, which says, "For thus saith the Lord: Ye shall not see wind, nor shall ye see rain; yet that valley shall be filled with water, that ye may drink, both ye and your cattle and your beasts". I knew things were settled in the spiritual realm. Although I could not see what was happening, God was working behind the scenes. All I knew was that it was going to end in praise.

I continued on the journey by faith, seeking God's face in my own little way, and learned to trust in God every moment of my life. I remembered 2 Corinthians 4:18, which says, "while we look not at the things which are seen, but at the things which are not seen, For the things which are seen are temporal, but the things which are not seen are eternal". So, I continued to believe this rhema that what I was seeing, and the condition of my daughter was temporary. The restoration I had not seen was eternal and permanent. Indeed, I began to call those things that were not as though they were. I began to decree according to Job 22:28: "Thou shalt also decree a thing, and it shall be established unto thee; and the light shall shine upon thy ways." I kept confessing positively and declaring what I wanted to happen, while I waged war in the spirit every midnight.

Most importantly, whether we believe it or not, there is power in the spoken Word, and I am a living witness. The Bible says whatever we bind on earth is bound in Heaven, and whatever we lose on earth is loosed in Heaven (Mathew 18:18). I held on to this Word and believed it with all my heart. You could tell that my life was dependent on the Word of God. When I looked at my baby's condition and felt demoralised, the Spirit of God reminded me that the condition was temporary, and the healing not seen was permanent. This became a big consolation for me as the days passed by. The Bible tells us that Jesus learned obedience from the things He suffered, and I learned to trust and draw faith from things I encountered. To trust God, we must believe He is trustworthy. According to the Oxford Dictionary, we trust someone when we believe they are honest, truthful, dependable, reliable, honourable, incorruptible, steadfast, unfailing, or faithful. Do all these words describe God and His nature? Absolutely! The Biblical definition of trust, based on the Hebrew word 'batah,' means

LIFE IN THE INTENSIVE CARE UNIT

to have confidence, to be secure in. When we trust in God, we believe and have confidence in His truths and abilities.

We believe that what His Word says about Him is true and unchangeable. This was my stand on this journey since I had no other option but to trust and have faith. My trust in God gave me the assurance to believe God will fulfil every promise He makes to us and that every Word He says is true. Putting faith into action by trusting in His power and attributes can sometimes be a challenge. Trying circumstances can leave us questioning God's plan, but with the help of the Holy Spirit, I forged ahead. Even though we all know that God is capable, we still allow fear, worry, or denial to get in the way of trusting Him fully. We need to be "all-in" and unwavering in our trust in God. I love these words by C. S. Lewis because it perfectly describes the push and pull of trusting God. None of us wants to go through tough times. Unfortunately, "in this world, you will have trouble."(John 16:33). Jesus wants us to claim His peace in our struggles, knowing He will always walk with us. Learning how to develop trust in God can be difficult sometimes, but it is not an impossible task.

There's great power in trusting Him. It clears the way for our security to be based solely on Him, not on our circumstances, or other people, not on ourselves, nor our own ways of thinking. The power of trusting God brings joy, protection,

BACK FROM THE DEAD

peace, comfort, and confidence. When we put our lives completely in His hands, we discard our tendency to trust in ourselves, others, or our circumstances. The alternative to trusting God is a life filled with anxiety, anger, doubts, and resentment. We must make a conscious effort to work on this process of trust. It will take effort and time, but it will bring a much better quality of life, which is what Jesus desires for us.

CHAPTER 2

TRUSTING THE GREAT PHYSICIAN

"The Great Physician" is one of Jesus' significant attributes. He came to this planet to heal humanity, and all four Gospels state healing as an essential element of Jesus' life. Jesus is and will always be the same healer He was over two thousand years ago. The following story concludes with Jesus' comments explaining His mission. Jesus and His disciples shared a supper at Matthew's house. Matthew gathered his friends, who were fellow tax collectors, as well as those considered sinners by the self-righteous Pharisees. Eating with them made them ceremonially "unclean," and the Pharisees questioned the followers about their Rabbi's activities. When Jesus heard them, He said In Matthew 9:1,

BACK FROM THE DEAD

"It is not the healthy who need a doctor, but the sick". This is the main reason Jesus came to us as both totally human and fully God.

We are all afflicted with the sickness of sin. It is a lethal sickness with only one cure. Only Jesus has the potent prescription we require. His death on the cross is a replacement for the penalty our sin deserves. He is our Great Physician and the Healer of our greatest sickness. In my challenge and desperation, I clung to the great physician, asking Him to appear for me night after night. I reminded Him of every promise I was aware of. It got to the point where I was conversing with the Holy Spirit virtually every minute. I became aware of His presence and referred to Him as my Helper, Comforter, and Trusted Friend. I pondered the Bible and asked myself if God could cure the leper, the blind, the dumb, the misshapen and the crippled, what about His daughter, a gift that He gave me that adds no sorrow? Jesus Himself asked, "can a mother forget her suckling child"? He added that even if she does, He would not forget us. He cured fevers, people who were maimed, paralyzed people, and many others of whom we are unaware! My case would not be an exception!

There are numerous accounts in the Old Testament about God's healing. God tells the Israelites that He will be their Jehovah Rapha, the God who heals (Exodos 15:26).

TRUSTING THE GREAT PHYSICIAN

The Israelites began to complain after their first three days in the desert. God had just opened the Red Sea for them, but they had short memories. God told the Israelites that if they listened to Him and obeyed His commands, He would not bring any of the diseases He had inflicted upon the Egyptians (Deuteronomy 7:15) upon them. He is saying the same to us today. If we trust and obey, we will eat the fruits of the land. Trusting God offers serenity and joy; relying on God brings faith and trust. Jesus heals the spirit, the soul, and the body. God's Word says in Exodus 15:26b,"For I am the Lord, who heals you." Subsequently, Matthew 8:16-17 says, "When evening came, many who were demon-possessed were brought to him, and he drove out the spirits with a word and healed all the sick". This was to fulfil what the prophet Isaiah said: "He took up our infirmities and carried our illnesses". Why then should mine be different? I held unto these words and continued to look unto Him.

According to the Bible, all our illnesses, be they physical, mental, or spiritual, are the result of man's initial sin and the curse that followed. When Jesus arrives with healing, God demonstrates that Jesus is the only one who can heal the affliction. Just as Jesus physically and emotionally healed everyone who came to Him, His sacrifice for our salvation is a once-and-for-all remedy for the sin that makes us sick. He is available 24 hours a day, seven days a week. He is always

BACK FROM THE DEAD

"on call," with no appointment required, so that we may be healed by His wounds. His services are provided without charge. He paid for everything. Knowing that Jesus had already paid the price for me, I knew my case was settled with Him.

God also provides us with the "medicine" of His Word to cure our unbelief, broken hearts, loneliness, emotional wounds, sadness, and sicknesses. As a man, Jesus experienced emotional, physical, and spiritual agony. He understands all our anguish. Is there anything in your life that needs God's healing? Jesus Christ our Jehovah Rapha, the God of Healing, continues to heal today.

God desires for us to be healed in all facets of our lives. Whatever ails us, we can reach out and put our trust in His kind and trustworthy care. Did you observe how Jesus never condemned anyone who came to him for healing? Today, the same is true. Romans 8:1 says, "There is therefore no condemnation for those who are in Christ Jesus." Jesus does not want to judge you. He wants to make you full and flawless in His eyes. So, His words calmed me, and all of these words kept me going day after day. I felt that the same Jesus who healed multitudes during His earthly ministry is still healing now. He understands our anguish and promises to always be by our side. We are never beyond His healing power. Healing can occur through the eradication of our bodily and mental

TRUSTING THE GREAT PHYSICIAN

illnesses, or in any other way that He decides. Psalm 23:4 says, "Even though I walk through the valley of the shadow of death, I will fear no evil, because you are with me; your rod and your staff, they comfort me".

From experience, sometimes, healing requires patience and trusting God consistently, but it can also happen instantly, and no matter when it happens, we can always believe in His timing. We tolerate pain because it causes us to rely on and draw closer to God. He utilizes time to shape us into His likeness. He also wants us to desire Him, the Healer, more than the healing He provides. God wants to heal every wound in our heart, mind, body, and soul. We must, however, pray for healing in faith, trust, and dependence, knowing that He has the final say and that it is always within His will. When we do not understand, we must trust. Even when He says no, trust that He is always good. The Bible says in Proverbs 3:5-6, "Lean not on your own understanding, but trust in the Lord with all your heart. Recognise Him in all your ways, and He will make your paths straight". Choose to be confident and secure in the person of God with everything you have. Bring your problems and decisions to Him in prayer, utilize His Word as a guide, and then follow Him down the route He has chosen for you.

To me, the story of Abraham and Isaac represents the peak of trust. God had promised Abraham a son, and the promise

BACK FROM THE DEAD

was fulfilled when he was one hundred years old. Isaac was born to Sarah. "Sometime later" (Genesis 22:1), God instructed Abraham to take Isaac and offer him as a burnt offering.

Abraham obeyed all of God's instructions, but just as he was about to kill his son, God intervened and saved Isaac. Abraham had a strong faith in God's ability to provide for him. He trusted Him to resurrect Isaac if necessary. He declared in Genesis 22:8: "God Himself will provide the lamb".

Jochebed, Moses' mother, trusted God to protect her son's life. They were slaves in Egypt, and Pharaoh, fearful of the Hebrews' prolific birth rate, ordered that all infant males born be killed. Jochebed, the mother of Moses, hid him for three months before placing him in the river in a waterproof basket, with his sister watching from a distance. Pharaoh's daughter discovered Moses, and Moses' sister raced in to offer to find him a nurse. Pharaoh's daughter agreed, and Jochebed was not only reunited with her son, but she was also paid to nurse him! Jochebed believed that God would utilize her efforts to save her baby boy, who later led the Israelites out of slavery.

Shadrach, Meshach, and Abednego, three Hebrew men, disobeyed King Nebuchadnezzar's instructions to bow down and worship his golden statue. They believed God would save them and were willing to give up their lives rather than serve

TRUSTING THE GREAT PHYSICIAN

any other god than their own. They not only survived but emerged absolutely unscathed after being bound and tossed in a burning furnace.

We do not totally trust people we do not know or with whom we have never spoken to. We must first get to know them. Prayer is the most effective approach to communicating with God and getting closer to Him. We pray to Him, and He responds through His Spirit, Scripture, natural wonders, our friends, Christian music, and even strangers. In my hospital experience, I heard God in every way possible.

When you are desperate to hear Him, you will absolutely hear Him.

CHAPTER 3

HOPE UPON IMPACT

One of the many lessons I learned from my hospital experience was that when families and close friends are caring for someone who is seriously ill, it is crucial to consider their own needs as well. I remembered entirely forgetting about my own needs so much so, that the medical staff were concerned about my mental health, but I was concerned about my child. There are numerous potential causes of exhaustion for carers who neglect their own well-being. These may include long distance travel, spending extended periods of time at the bedside of loved ones, experiencing anxiety, inadequate nutrition due to lack of appetite, and insufficient sleep. It is therefore critical, that we look after ourselves when we care for others.

HOPE UPON IMPACT

I recall when my uncle's wife became extremely ill, and her husband died of exhaustion while caring for his wife. I can also recollect occasions in which the provider died before the person receiving care. Sometimes, the carer gets sick soon after the death of their loved one.

Occasionally, even when hospitals offer on-site accommodation or lists of reasonably priced hotels, some family members choose to spend the night in the hospital, either because they live far away or because they want to be close to their loved ones. Some spend every second with the patient, frightened that it would be their last, and appreciate being allowed to stay at the hospital, even if it is only in a chair next to the patient's bedside. This might be harmful. I have been there. Carers need to be deliberate about taking care of themselves in addition to their loved ones. From my experience, the people who work in the ICU do an excellent job. This team of medical specialists cares for patients who mostly have tubes and cables hooked to a myriad of bleeping monitors and ventilators. However, as I observed the nurses turn my motionless baby around, tears streamed down my cheeks, yet I praised God for His faithfulness and her perfect health.

My days in the hospital had become routine; nurses, physicians, consultants, and surgeons came in and went like angels, providing constant care for my child. Whenever, I saw

BACK FROM THE DEAD

the medical team approaching, I prayed against a negative report. Having overheard the doctor describe my baby's condition and the upcoming procedure at two weeks old was the first depressing experience I had. I trembled at the thought but reminded myself to take it one step at a time.

As a distractive technique, I took pictures of the toys by her bed, the view outside her window, and anything else that connected her with her environment in an attempt to better understand myself as these were all priceless memories for me. I nuzzled my baby's downy cheek, smelled her hair, and held her hands whenever I was given the opportunity to have contact with her, though just for few minutes, and we would be separated again. The opportunity to touch her came very rarely due to all the equipment and tubes she was linked with.

As I observed the situation, combined with the doctor's unfavourable diagnosis, it did not give me optimism in any way. However, I gained courage from God's Word because I understood that everything I saw was temporary, but the healing I could not see with my physical eyes was eternal.

One thing I have realized is that no matter what condition we are in, we may boldly come before God and lay all at His feet. Whatever we consider impossible, is possible with God because He has no bounds nor boundaries. Everything is possible because of His might. When life appears difficult, we can cling to His promises. Isaiah 58:11a says, "The Lord will guide you always."

God is with you even in the most difficult circumstances.

Isaiah 43:2 says, "When you pass through the waters, I will be with you; and when you pass through the rivers, they will not sweep over you. You will not be harmed if you walk into the fire; the flames will not set you ablaze".

He is on our side and has the final say. Romans 8:31 says, "What shall we then say to these things?" Who can be against us if God is for us"?

We have already seen in God's Word an immaculate conception, a miraculous pregnancy in a menopausal woman, and our deliverance from sin. What about the implausible instances of God speaking the universe into being? Or how about David, the young soldier, taking down a nine-foot-tall goliath with a slingshot and a rock? How about God splitting the Red Sea, allowing the Israelites to flee from the Egyptian army and reaching safety? For 40 years, He fed two million people manna and quail. What about Daniel, for whom God shut the mouths of the lions? That was Old Testament, right? What about the five thousand people Jesus fed with five loaves of bread and two fishes? Wow, His miracles are too many to list. God raising Jesus from the dead shows that His creative power and provision for His people is real. It also indicates that He does some of His best work when things appear impossible for us.

I believe we serve a God of all impossibility, yet anxiety and fear could creep into our faith. I know He is a loving and sovereign God. Though, the mountain in front of us may appear insurmountable and unfair at times, we must remember to turn to His Word for guidance. From the Bible, when the angel notified Mary of her upcoming pregnancy and the birth of the Messiah; she sought clarification on what appeared to be an impossible possibility. The angel reassured her further, informing her that her elderly relative Elizabeth was also pregnant. This evidence of God's great strength was followed by the assurance that nothing is impossible for God.

In addition, Jesus made a similar statement at the end of the story of the rich young ruler. He narrated the obstacles that a wealthy man experiences before entering the kingdom of heaven. This idea astonished the disciples because they believed God bestowed numerous blessings on the wealthy, including salvation. "Who then can be saved"? they asked. (Matthew 19:25). Jesus assured them that all things are possible with God. Jesus tells us we are God's own descriptions of the magnificent way in which His Word works. "As rain and snow fall from heaven and do not return without watering the earth and making it bud and flourish, yielding seed for the Sower and bread for the eater, so is my word that goes forth from my mouth: it will not return to me empty, but will accomplish what I desire and achieve the purpose for which I sent it" (Isaiah 55:10 -11).

Rain and snow are part of a cyclical process of precipitation that falls from the skies to the earth and enters the soil, allowing crops to flourish and the hungry to be fed. God compares His Word to rain and snow because it comes from Him and falls on us to refresh, grow, and feed our souls. For me, the most amazing aspect is that when He breathes forth His Word and we take it in, it is always for a clear purpose. It achieves what He desires. Have you ever read a "verse of the day" and felt as if it was speaking directly to you? Have you ever had a verse spring to mind out of nowhere? This does not happen by accident. It is the power of His Word. It bears fruit in our lives as we take it in, word by word, inspired by the Holy Spirit. We acquire serenity, comfort, guidance, and delight as we continue to grow in His wisdom and understanding. Every minute and every second we spend in His Word has a great purpose!

In the gospel of John, after a particularly difficult teaching, Jesus said to the disciples, "The words I have spoken to you are spirit, and they are life". (John 6:63).

BACK FROM THE DEAD

Just as we must consume food to survive, we must also consume the Word of God and receive it in our hearts and souls, so that it can have a positive impact on our lives. The Holy Spirit dwells within us and brings His words "alive". Power lies in its ability to sustain life. According to Matthew 4:4, we live by God's Word. It says, "Man shall not live by bread alone, but by every word that comes from the mouth of God."

When Jesus delivered these words to the devil, He was quoting Deuteronomy 8:3, reminding him of the manna God provided for the Israelites. The purpose of the manna was to humble them and teach them that "man does not live on bread alone, but on every Word that comes from the mouth of the Lord".

Similarly, Job took this directive to heart. He said, "I have treasured His words more than anything else". Is His Word more valuable than the food you consume? While we rarely skip a meal, we sometimes consider time spent reading His Word to be optional in our lives. Other actions are prioritized above it in importance. We cannot believe everything we read on the internet or hear from news outlets. Note that everyone seems to have their own set of information, opinions, and statistics, but no matter how sophisticated our human comprehension is, it is nothing compared to God's wisdom. It is worth knowing that in a world full of lies and empty

HOPE UPON IMPACT

promises, His Word provides us with the ultimate power and wisdom to live a life of victory.

CHAPTER 4

AND MY BABY DIED

So, after a while in the hospital, I decided it was time to go home and see my other children as I had left them to look after my one missing child. This reminds me of the parable of the lost sheep, in Matthew 18:12 and Luke 15:4 about a compassionate shepherd who abandons his ninety-nine sheep in search of one that has gone missing. This demonstrates the importance of everyone in the family, especially those who are vulnerable. No wonder Jesus says He came for the sick, for it is the sick that require a physician. Jesus has rescued me, redeemed me, and brought me into His family forever. What about you? When you believe in Him and accept His sacrifice, you are perfect in His eyes! It is so important to know your identity in Jesus! Do not let the world,

AND MY BABY DIED

other people, or even your own thoughts tell you otherwise. None of us are worthy of His love, but He gives it freely. Also, with that comes the Holy Spirit within us to help us, guide us, and give us His wisdom.

Thankfully, I have no fear because I am a member of Jesus' family, my courage comes from Him, and all the promises regarding His healing power are mine. And this is my faith in Him. Though things may not go the way I want them to sometimes, I know they are settled in my heart because of my trust in God. According to the Bible, when the enemy comes like a flood, Jesus will raise a standard against him. The Bible teaches me that I should not be fearful nor discouraged. I am aware of who I am. According to the songwriter, Sinach who says, "I am working in power, I am working in miracles because I know who I am". This is what I believe, and I have never been disappointed. The Bible says that God's Word is yes and amen, which means it is true and real. The Word of God is my light and salvation; who can say it, and have it come true if the Lord has not commanded it? The Bible says I am more than a conqueror and that God has given me the power to destroy the works of the devil. So, when I recalled God's words in that situation, I felt that the battle was already won because I fought from the point of victory.

Then again, as I walked across the hospital parking lot that day, my mind raced, my heart was heavy, and I was

BACK FROM THE DEAD

overwhelmed with all the stress I was going through. I felt completely alone and helpless, despite my faith in God. Just to clarify, even as a Christian, fear and anxiety are inevitable, but how they are handled is what matters. For an unbeliever, it is very easy to be overwhelmed with fear and anxiety, which could lead to other diseases. However, for a believer, the Word of God sets us free immediately. This is our advantage in Christ Jesus, that when we are faced with the impossible, we speak out the Word and stand on the Rock that never fails. The Psalmist says in Psalm 56:3, "When I am afraid, I put my trust in you".

We can pray and wait patiently with expectation, as the Bible says in Psalm 5:3: "In the morning, I lay my requests before you and wait in expectation".

In addition, we can praise and worship God in the midst of adversity. Paul and Silas were imprisoned even though they were innocent of any crime. They endured being beaten and put in stocks in a cell deep in the bowels of a prison. Their situation must have seemed dire as they struggled in pain and were locked away despite their innocence. What did they do in this impossible situation? They praised and worshiped God.

Acts 16:25-26 recounts that "about midnight, Paul and Silas were praying and singing hymns to God, and the other prisoners were listening to them. Suddenly, there was such a

AND MY BABY DIED

violent earthquake that the foundations of the prison were shaken. At once all the prison doors flew open, and everybody's chains came loose". This is the work of the Holy Spirit.

Consequently, we can build our confidence in God. I have previously mentioned the story of David and Goliath. David confronted Goliath, a seemingly insurmountable obstacle, due to his unwavering faith and confidence in God. He defeated Goliath through the application of his faith and assurance in God. In the face of the impossible, we can have confidence that God can perform the miraculous. Never doubt the God of the impossible. Pray and believe, for God can accomplish everything. He is unstoppable. We worship a powerful God. Yes, we serve a mighty God. Allow Him to show you His mighty power and glory!

Ephesians 3:20 says, "Now to him who is able to do immeasurably more than we ask or imagine, according to his power that is at work within us, to him be glory in the church and in Christ Jesus throughout all generations, forever and ever! Amen".

So, keep praying! and set time aside to speak to God about the situation, and then really listen for His response, for He will surely speak.

Returning to my testimony, as I arrived home to see my other

BACK FROM THE DEAD

children, the doctor contacted me and enquired if I had spoken to my spouse. I stated that we had seen each other before he departed for work that morning. The doctor questioned if my husband had told me anything new. No, I said. She said, "OK, I'll wait for your husband to tell you". I advised that because she was already on the phone with me, she could as well provide the information. She replied, "No, we'll wait for your husband to contact you". I persisted, and she said, "your baby just died a few minutes ago, she's lying lifeless right now". "No way!", I said; this is not God's promise to me. God stated that I would not cast my children before their time, and the doctor said she was sorry I needed to contact my husband right away for help.

At that point, the doctor got concerned about my mental health and began to enquire whether I had someone with me at home and if I needed assistance or some sort of counselling. "No, this is not what God told me", I yelled. God said, "My baby will not die; she will live to show forth God's glory". The doctor became further confused and baffled, 'I will send someone to support you as soon as possible', she stuttered.

As soon as she hung up the phone, the Holy Spirit told me, "This is not the time for wailing and crying; gather your strength because you are on the battlefield". At that point, I could not pray again and did not know what to do because my

AND MY BABY DIED

baby had died in the midst of all the spiritual exercises. Amidst all, the Holy Spirit reminded me that what I heard now was only temporary, and to refer to those things that were not as though they were (Romans 4:17). The Spirit impressed on me that death and life are in the power of the tongue, and I should confess with my mouth the miracle I needed (Proverbs 18:21). With my mouth, I began to announce that my baby would not die but would live to praise God. I also recalled Pastor Adeboye, the general overseer of the Redeemed Christian Church of God, who had said if prayer failed, try praise.

In despair, I remembered Job's story, how it shows us his honest struggles through great suffering and his faith to make it through impossible situations. After all his difficulties, Job finally tells God, "I know that you can do all things; no plan of yours can be thwarted". (Job 42:2). Job did not understand why he had to go through these things, but we see in his story that he clung to what he knew about God. His faith and trust kept him going through the struggle. This was such a great comfort to me! I needed to hold on tight to the truths of God's character, abilities, and love for me in the impossible situation.

Also, I have come to realise that our faith is not intellectual knowledge or facts. It is a gift from God. When Paul was discussing being a living sacrifice, he taught us how to live out our saving faith. He said, in Romans 12:3b, "think of yourself with sober judgment, in accordance with the measure of faith

BACK FROM THE DEAD

God has given you".

We all have a "measure of faith" given to us that drew us to Jesus, and we expand and deepen our faith by hearing and reading the Word of God. Romans 10:17 says, "So then faith comes by hearing, and hearing the word of God". Likewise, Jesus needed His disciples to know how important their faith would be for their upcoming ministry. In the Parable of the Mustard Seed, the disciples could not heal a demon-possessed boy. After Jesus healed the boy, the disciples came to Him and asked why they could not heal him. He said to them in Matthew 17:20: "Because you have so little faith. I tell you the truth, if you have faith as small as a mustard seed, you can say to this mountain, 'Move from here to there' and it will move. Nothing will be impossible for you".

To do the impossible, we all require unwavering faith in God and complete humility. Jesus wants us to believe in our hearts and minds that He can do anything. He wants us to have a mustard seed of faith, not a mustard seed of doubt! We have all the proof we need to believe in Jesus and His capabilities. We know His Word and promises are true. The written record and testimony of the early believers exist for our benefit.

Permit me to say that faith in God is a life-saving power. It is not a feeling. No, it is a belief in the power of God, and when we lay hold of faith, we experience the tremendous power to change our lives completely. Living a life of faith changed my

AND MY BABY DIED

life completely in many ways. Please allow me to share a few with you.

1. I no longer need to worry about the future.

"Be anxious for nothing," Paul encourages us in Philippians 4:6. Peter 5:7 says we need to believe wholly in God, "Casting all your care upon Him, for He cares for you".

If we trust only as far as we understand, then we have every reason to worry about the various trials and hardships that come our way. After all, we don't know what their purpose is. We don't know what the outcome will be, or what long-term effect it will have on us. And as for the future? There is a whole lifetime of unseen circumstances over which we could drive ourselves mad with fretting.

But if we choose to have faith, and trust in God, the Master Builder who guides everything in heaven and on earth, then we are freed from worrying about our lives. God has a perfect plan for us in everything He sends our way. Trials and tests come our way so that when we overcome, the virtues of Jesus can grow in us. God already knows the outcome since His Word was sent forth before we encountered the difficulty; all we have to do is declare God's Word in opposition to the difficulty, there will be freedom. We can cast all our care on Him and focus our energy on God. He has lovingly and carefully planned out our entire lives. We have to sincerely believe that we do not have any reason to be anxious about everything past, present, and future.

2. Living a life of faith makes me strong, confident, and brave.

The truth is, if we muddle along in our own strength, without faith in God, we will quickly fall into despair when we are faced with shortcomings. However, if we have faith in God and the power of His Word, we know that we do not have to survive by our own strength. God will surely show up. I am a living witness.

2 Chronicles 2:19 says, "For the eyes of the Lord run to and fro throughout the whole earth, to show Himself strong on behalf of those whose heart is loyal to Him".

There is also this incredible promise in Romans 16:20: "And the God of peace will crush Satan under your feet shortly".

If we have faith in these verses, and in all of the scriptures, we will be confident even in our trials. We will be fully assured that God will crush Satan under our feet. The outcome is certain! God will show Himself strong on our behalf, and victory is sure. Faith will make us strong and bold in our battle against sin and calamities. This was the secret I employed in my battle with the devil.

3. Living a life of faith gives me joy and victory.

"Being confident of this very thing, that He who has begun a good work in you will complete it until the day of Jesus Christ". (Philippian 1:6).

God has started a work in us, and this brings incredible joy to each one who longs to be part of Jesus's family. And not only has God begun a work, but we are also assured that He will complete it. God does not begin something and then drop it or lose interest halfway through. If we have faith in God's Word, in His promises to transform us, and in His power to help us overcome issue, then we will be filled with joy. This is why I make myself happy all of the time, and not even the devil will be allowed to steal my joy from me.

4. Living a life of faith makes me immovable.

Psalm 125 says, "Those who trust in the Lord are like Mount Zion, which cannot be moved, but abides forever".

In several places in the Bible, God's Word is compared to a rock. In the gospel of Matthew, Jesus tells us that whoever hears His sayings and does them, will be like a man who built his house on rock. And no matter what storms come and beat against that house, it will remain standing, because of the solid foundation of faith on which it is built, (Matthew 7:24 - 27). Conversely, those who live by their feelings and put their trust in things of this earth are like a man who builds his house on sand. The first storm will take that house down. By believing in God and choosing to live by faith, and not by feelings, which are as changeable as the weather itself, we stand immovable in the storms of life. Nothing can cause us to become discouraged. Nothing can steal our faith because we believe in the almighty God. This has helped me in numerous conflicts, as I remained unyielding throughout the storm.

5. Living a life of faith produces miracles.

The Old Testament is filled with stories of people who experienced miracles through the power of faith. Think about David. Though he was a young boy, he believed without a doubt that God would help him overcome the giant Goliath. He did not rationalize to work out how much bigger than him the giant was, or how many more years of battle experience he had. He chose to believe in God, and he went ahead in faith. As a result of his faith, he saved the Israelite army from the Philistines! There are countless other examples of miracles God has performed. We should learn to be thankful instead of complaining. If we believe in God, that miracle will take place right inside of us, and the evidence will show forth. Hebrew 11:39-40 says, "And all these, having obtained a good testimony through faith, did not receive the promise,

AND MY BABY DIED

God having provided something better for us, that they should not be made perfect apart from us". Peter 1:3-4 puts it succinctly:

"As His divine power has given to us all things that pertain to life and godliness, through the knowledge of Him who called us by glory and virtue, by which have been given to us exceedingly great and precious promises, that through these you may be partakers of the divine nature, having escaped the corruption that is in the world through lust".

CHAPTER 5

GRATITUDE IN GRIEF

So, as the doctor hung up the phone after delivering the bad news, I began to sing and dance, which turned into thanksgiving in grief. My only hope was to dance and praise God since I didn't know what else to do. This went on till dusk, when I ran out of energy to keep going and fell asleep unintentionally. I leapt up minutes later, feeling so horrible that I slept off after learning that my baby had died. I burst into tears and tried hard not to cry because I did not want my other children to understand what was going on. How would I have conveyed to my children, who had been praying with me for their sister, that she had died? So, I quickly wiped my tears and proceeded to worship God until I ran out of strength the second time. By this time, it was already late. My husband had come back and wanted me to take it easy as I looked so exhausted, with no water or food for the whole day. He asked me what he could do to help me, and I asked him to step aside and allow me to warfare all night. My husband felt deeply sorry for me and did not know what to do to help me because I was like an angry lion ready to devour anyone who told me anything contrary to what God revealed to me.

After my praise and worship, I meditated on God's Word, which never fails. I reflected on all the battles God had fought for me and the victories that ensued. I reassured myself that this would be one of them. I also realized that in so many instances in the Bible where there were difficulties, the Bible came back to say, "And it came to pass". So, I encouraged myself that this event would likewise come to pass. Nevertheless, I worshiped and concentrated on God's Word until the morning. I hurriedly dropped the kids off with a caregiver and headed straight to the hospital. When I arrived at the hospital the next day, my baby had already been placed on life support, and I was told that if her heart did not restart after three days, they would have to remove the machine. I reassured the doctor that her heart had already revived, and that the life support could be removed with the help and might of the Holy Spirit.

However, everyone, including the health professionals, thought I was not making sense and that I needed help. I tried

BACK FROM THE DEAD

to explain myself to them, that it was not me speaking but the Holy Spirit's conviction, but this seemed futile. The doctors had already concluded that my daughter would not survive, but I reassured them that she would live and not die. All through the first day, they were very unsure about her recovery. On the second day, we were told that they would remove the life support and that she had a 50/50 chance of survival. I told them that she would live and not die. In fact, I knew she was already living. On the third day, I continued to encourage the doctors to remove the life support as I was convinced that my daughter was alive.

Apparently, the medical practitioners did not want me to be present when they removed the equipment, so that they could swiftly take her to the morgue before I arrived and inform me that they could not have left her all night because of other patients. However, they had no idea of the assurance I had received from the Holy Spirit. At 2 a.m. on that same day, they dismantled the machine, and alas, my baby was alive! When I arrived at the hospital that morning, I praised God, but they told me it was not time to rejoice yet, that it would take three days before they could certify that she would live. I told them that my baby would live forever. I went around and prophesied unto her, and I stayed with her all day.

One thing that encourages me about God is that He sees us in our situation and circumstance. He said He has engraved

GRATITUDE IN GRIEF

us upon the palm of His hands (Isaiah 49:16). God knew what our lives would be like, trials that would want to steal our joy, hardships that would want to steal our comfort, and pressures that would want to steal our peace. In spite of all, our first choice should always be His Word. He loves and cares for us dearly and equips us with the power of His Word to empower us to have a joy-filled and peaceful life. Reading God's Word meets all our needs. Each Word is inspired by God and is absolute truth. God reveals His heart and mind to us through His Word. His Word is a blessing to those who richly dwell in it. We will not live forever, but God's Word is eternal and unfailing. In the words of Isaiah 40:8, "The grass withers and the flowers fall, but the word of our God stands forever".

God's Word transforms our lives and shows us lasting solutions to every problem and need. His Word ignites a passion to know Him fully and hear His voice. The Bible tells us that God used only the power of His Word to speak our entire world into being. Jesus calmed the storm, healed the sick, and cast out demons with His Words. God's Word overcomes the world, and He graciously gives His Word to us. This is the importance of treasuring the Word and spending time in His presence daily. Going through all of this, God's Word was my comfort, reassurance, and conviction all through the journey. Trusting God in the face of adversity is crucial but also very difficult. Trusting God when everything

BACK FROM THE DEAD

seems to be failing and there is nothing positive to hold on to is very challenging. This reminds me of the story of Haggai in Genesis 16, when she thought it was time for her and her child to die, but God saw her and made provision for her. Our God sees us and makes provision for us behind the scenes.

At that point, nothing meant more to me than my baby's life as she remained a patient at the hospital. Having a baby in the intensive care unit can be one of the most difficult and challenging experiences of life. As I waited for the day when my baby was ready to come home with me, my life appeared empty without her. I reflected that we had not spent time together apart from when she was in the womb and immediately when she was born. I needed to show her the love of a mother to a child, I needed to cuddle her in my arms and breastfeed her. At the thought of all, I concluded that I was willing to persevere in my warfare for her survival. I had left the other children at home and spent all my time with her. Little wonder then, when Jesus says that if a man has 100 sheep and loses one, he will abandon the other 99 to go after the lost one. This is a true saying because my attitude was that others were healthy and did not need me as much as my angel at the hospital. Furthermore, I had asked myself why I needed the money in my bank account when I could easily give it to churches and charities as a thanksgiving offering, who knows, God could show me mercy.

GRATITUDE IN GRIEF

I received the idea from Benny Hinn, who stated in one of his speeches that the day he sowed into his father-in-law and other men of God, doors opened for him. So, I persuaded myself that if I sowed into charity, maybe God would show me mercy. I then sent something substantial, known as a thanksgiving offering, to the churches. I purposefully avoided requesting prayers, instead expressing gratitude for God's mercy. It also indicates that in tough times, our giving is a sacrifice, and God may offer us mercy for it.

Notably, I recall reading a book that says the world is made up of two sets of people: those who live with fear and those who live on purpose and for a great purpose in faith. Those who live with faith have hope. Hope is found in the reality that the Lord delights in turning impossible situations into opportunities to show His amazing love for people. The story of Zechariah, in the book of Luke, gives us an insight into what hope looks like when all seems lost. Zachariah and his wife Elizabeth were old and had no offspring and faced an impossible situation. However, God made a way for them. Here are three lessons to instil hope in impossible situations from the story of my daughter.

BACK FROM THE DEAD

1. Our impossible situations set the stage for the Lord to do His work.

People have seemingly impossible circumstances facing them in one way or the other. It may be stress from children, illness, marriage turmoil, finances, or addiction. Zechariah and Elizabeth faced a physical impossibility of having a child. Regardless of the circumstances we face, they all set the stage for Jesus to show His infinite power and grace! God is unpredictable. In fact, God appears to specialize in surprises, particularly the impossible. We frequently expect Him to do one thing and He does another. We expect Him to move in one direction, yet He frequently moves in another.

Sometimes we trust Him to handle something right away, and He waits for when He knows is right. Also, there were instances when we expected to wait longer, and He showed up and solved what appeared to be an impossible situation almost overnight. God enjoys doing things over which we have no control, and He has designed our lives in this manner. What we consider impossible, God sees as a non-issue. Matthew 19:26 says, "With men this is impossible, but with God all things are possible". Luke 1:37 says, "For nothing will be impossible with God". Nothing, not even the most overwhelming obstacle, will be impossible to overcome with God. God prefers to work in situations that you consider "impossible." When we throw up our hands and say, "There is no other way," God delights in proving Himself to be God. In my daughter's case, even the doctors thought her condition was hopeless, but God showed up for us because we trusted in Him.

2. The Lord's delays are not necessarily His denials.

We can often misinterpret waiting as a "no" from God. Zechariah and Elizabeth must have wondered if God had said no to their plea for a child. God's timing and method always differ from our own. Rather than allowing these moments to cause us to doubt, we can use them as a means for growth by setting aside impatience and anger with reassurance from the truths the Holy Spirit reminds us of. I notice something very interesting in Luke 1:5: "In the days of Herod, king of Judea, there was a certain priest named Zacharias". Notice the phrase "a certain priest". In the midst of the darkness, discouragement, and depression of an era when God seemed to be silent for the rest of time, God slipped onto the scene of this earth and pointed to an ageing priest. His wife was an elderly woman with grey hair; she was barren, and they were both righteous in God's eyes, walking blamelessly through all the precepts and requirements of the law. Yet, they waited until God intervened in His own time. It is also worth noting that my daughter lived in the hospital for four months. During that time, it was easy to believe that God had forgotten about her, but we persisted through midnight warfare prayers, and daily fasting, making intercession everyday relentlessly.

3. When the Lord intervenes, His surprises are always for His immediate glory and ultimate good.

Contrary to popular opinion, the Lord does not operate as a heavenly Santa Claus. We made a mess of His world and ought to endure its consequences with no saving grace. However, God promised to intervene by becoming one like us in the person of Jesus Christ. When God gave Zechariah and Elizabeth a baby, He did so primarily for His glory and for their good. Romans 8:28 reminds us: that God "causes all things to work together for those who love God, for those who are called according to His purpose".

We have hope that God makes promises that He will always keep. As a result, we can set aside anxiety and worry about the future and give them to God. This was exactly what I did. I gave all the worry and anxiety to God to take care of and watched Him do the miraculous for my daughter.

Glory be to His holy name!

CHAPTER 6

GOD OF THE IMPOSSIBLE

A few of the influences that sustained me during that period of unending fasting and midnight warfare were my total dependence on God's Word and my unwavering focus on it. I had no contingency plan, all I needed was God's intervention and mercy. I also pondered on 2 Kings 19, the God of Hezekiah, and established that Hezekiah's illness was not for his death, but for the Lord's glory. I learned that God wished to be glorified in the life of my daughter. Whenever I had a sense of dread, I went straight to the Bible and read it until it made sense to me. We believe that God is supreme, that He knows everything about us, and that He has a wonderful plan for our lives. However, trusting God is sometimes easier said than done. Even though we know God's plans are always good, we may still find it difficult to trust Him in the face of adversity. How do we harness the power of trusting God when our circumstances do not make sense? "Yet, not as I will, but as you will". (Matthew 26:39).

After all, the doctors concluded, after much thought, that my daughter would require surgery to correct any abnormality. However, this did not sit well with our family, but we still trusted God because everything works together for good for those that trust God. Due to the urgent nature of the surgery, we were unable to engage in any form of physical or psychological preparation. Parents were normally given days or weeks to prepare for their child's operation, and dependent on the condition of their child, they met with surgeons at various times. While others scheduled meetings well in advance, we did not. Nevertheless, I am eternally grateful to the Holy Spirit, who consistently appears as an unannounced helpmate. The inspiration of the Holy Spirit made us feel adequately prepared, and we appreciated the surgeon's calm approach and description of the surgical procedure.

Generally, parents are often anxious before surgery. In what way would their children respond to the anaesthesia? A consent form was also required of parents, which many found challenging to approve. The consent form for our daughter's surgery required our signature, which also burdened us.

GOD OF THE IMPOSSIBLE

As parents, we never want to confront the fact that our children will experience their own difficulties. That just does not seem like something that should happen. They are so new to the world and so young that they cannot possibly face obstacles. Yet, we must also recognise that we live in an imperfect world where there are illnesses, obstacles, and uncertainties that affect even our children, whether they are babies or older children. As a result, we must continuously pray to God for our families. And in all, God has made a way of escape. It would have been quite upsetting to hand over the baby to the surgeons. However, we did not have to in our circumstance because our baby was already in the intensive care unit.

In the midst of stress and confusion in the world, thoughts can become dispersed, and we may not know where to begin. If feeling anxious and worried, remember the words of 1 Peter 5.7, which encourages to "cast all your anxiety on him, because he cares for you". If going through any challenge, remember His invitation in Psalm 50.15 to "call on me in the day of trouble, and I will deliver you, and you will honour me".

God is still a Healer who can, and frequently does, heal through medicine, surgery, or His Word. God continues to deliver people from straining situations. Remember, in Psalm 147:3, He assures us that "He binds up the broken-hearted and heals their wounds". So, trust God when He says in Jeremiah 30:17, "I will restore your health and heal your wounds".

As I continued to pray, supported by scripture, built upon a solid foundation in God's Word, I was inundated with God's comfort and peace that passes all understanding, not as the world gives, and the Holy Spirit performed His Word. On the day of the surgery, as I tried to be strong, emotions got the better of me. "We'll take good care of her", the nurse stated. My eyes welled up with tears until we saw the nurse disappear behind the double doors leading into the surgical centre with my daughter. I had some confidence in the procedure's overall safety. The Holy Spirit reassured me that everything would be fine, and He gave them instructions on how to prepare for the procedure. I was spiritually engaged but physically distant.

I cannot even begin to imagine how parents feel when their children require surgery or treatment. I can, however, relate to the feeling of powerlessness that came with knowing that my role ended the moment I went through the hospital doors that morning, and would continue until my baby was wheeled back into her bed. Therefore, I placed my trust in God. I assumed that my daughter was too young to understand what was going on. It is critical to remember that our children rely on us to make them feel protected. Some youngsters are

GOD OF THE IMPOSSIBLE

extremely emotionally sensitive and will sense if you are tense or anxious. Keeping our emotions in check, learning what to expect, and focusing on the positives will help us feel more at ease in any situation.

The surgery took hours, and then the recovery time began. We were transferred to the recovery ward, but that was just the start of our lengthy hospital stay. My baby grew sick from every formula or breast milk she was given on a daily basis. My baby would vomit every liquid that entered her mouth; no liquid remained in her stomach, and this continued without knowing the cause. The physicians became alarmed, and a series of tests were performed, all to no avail. Days passed with no evidence that my child was on the mend. I continued my midnight warfare prayer and was certain the battle had already been won. I became an evangelist in the ward. I preached on God's faithfulness. I made friends and was determined to focus on winning rather than on the problem, and remained convinced that one day we would return home with our child.

Another month passed, and there was no sign that we would leave anytime soon. Every possible test and examination had been performed by the doctors. Finally, the doctors believed that they must have left something in her after the operation. So, they wanted to operate a second time, which we objected

BACK FROM THE DEAD

to, but then we realized that because my child's condition was not improving, perhaps they were right. We agreed, and a second surgery was performed, but no new findings were made. The difficult issue was that no diagnosis was available for her. The doctors were not quite sure what was wrong.

At this point, I realised that certain illnesses lacked a diagnosis, and that in such cases, it could be challenging to administer medication. It is the worst thing that may happen to any individual. In the event that a diagnosis is made, the patient can see a doctor for prescription; otherwise, there is no cure. The doctors therefore carried out examination after examination so that the professionals could assess the condition. By then, we had been in the hospital for three months, and there seemed to be no chance of us getting out anytime soon. I arrived at the hospital first and left last among the parents whose children were receiving care. My extended hospital stay worried the nurses, who believed I required counselling, but I knew I needed God's intervention.

On this earth, we are all traveling to places we have never been before. There are also others who are feeling overwhelmed and challenged by life. And it might happen to any of us. But one thing we must remember is that nothing is too difficult for God. He is trustworthy and true in all things, no matter what the topic or scenario looks like. His vows will never be broken. Every Word He gives is released, and it enters into whatever He sent it for, and that thing is completed (Isaiah 55:11). God's strength never fails. God's power can never be surpassed. We live in a supernatural kingdom, and kingdom life requires us to say things that are not seen. It behoves us to look into the Spirit. It leads us to recognise that we serve a God who is greater than everything else and can do exceedingly and abundantly above and beyond what we ask or conceive, by dint of the power that works in us (Ephesians 5:20). The Holy Spirit is the source of that strength.

The power of Christ in us allows us to live out and demonstrate the way Jesus lived. And that power is still available to us now. God supports us more than we can possibly comprehend. All I want is for God to open our eyes to see how much He loves us, how much He is with us, and how much He is for us. No matter what is against us, the challenge, the difficulty, the battle, the chaos, all of society's discontent, the division that is occurring among people of all genders and ethnicities - the Bible states that God is greater than all these things. When God enters with His power, everything changes. With men, it may be impossible, but with God, everything is possible. There is nothing that God cannot accomplish. There is nothing greater than Him. He is a God

BACK FROM THE DEAD

who performs feats that astound us. Nothing is too difficult for Him. He wishes to demonstrate His love for us.

I was told the story of a young Christian lad who applied to two programs at his university that required extremely high grades, but instead of improving from the previous semester, his grades depreciated. He was well aware that his grades were far below what was required. He pleaded to God, explaining that he did not understand why his grades were lower than what was required. God knew that the major reason the youngster wanted to go to university was to pursue one of these degrees, and here he found himself unable to do so. This young man was stressed and heartbroken. Before applying, he gave it a serious thought because, in his opinion, and in reality, it did not make sense to apply if he did not meet the requirements.

However, he heard a voice urging him to apply regardless. Despite his reservations, he applied. This was a truly impossible position! He was watching videos of people testifying about how God turned impossible situations into possible ones. While fasting and begging for God to intercede in his circumstances, he was accepted into the program for which he was unqualified. This is what God is capable of. Sometimes, a long wait, unpleasant and exhausting delays, give us the time and space to strengthen our faith. It makes

GOD OF THE IMPOSSIBLE

no difference how tough or impossible it appears. The same God who divided the Red Sea to allow the Israelites to flee from the Egyptians is the same God today and forever. Therefore, He will make a way for you even when there appears to be none.

God wants us to believe He can do it. Faith begins when God's Will is understood. Knowing that God can do anything is the foundation of hope. Faith is founded on knowing God will do it. Some people do not believe it is possible to know God's Will. They do not believe that God speaks to people in a personal way. The truth is that He treats us the same way He treated individuals in the Old Testament, the New Testament, and, most notably, the Gospels. Jesus spoke personally to individuals and continues to do so through the Holy Spirit. God continues to communicate today, but we must seek Him until we hear Him. And when we do hear Him, we will understand His Will and He will have an answer for our situation.

Knowing the God that I serve, as I consistently prayed, God showed me the root cause of the unexplained illness. He revealed to me that my child was unable to hold on to fluids. When I learned about this revelation, I thought it was ridiculous as I couldn't understand how it could be the root cause of the unknown sickness. Nonetheless, I shared the revelation with one of the nurses, and she suggested that I inform the doctor. It was really hard for me to explain it to the doctor since, in all honesty, it did not make sense. How could the feeding catheter she was using to receive her food be the main source of concern, as revealed by the Holy Spirit?

Feeding catheters are medical devices used to feed people who are unable to eat or drink. Doctors push a needle through the skin into the vein and then thread a guide wire through the needle to position the catheter. After removing the needle, the catheter is passed over the guide wire, which is then removed. It is also known as intravenous feeding, and according to the doctor, my baby could not survive without it until she was able to eat and drink on her own.

Being aware of the importance of the feeding catheter, I asked the doctor if we could remove it and try conventional eating for a few hours. The doctor concluded that it would never happen except if I wanted my child dead because every formula or breast milk given would come out straight away.

I felt so devastated, as no one listened to me or understood the revelation. How could I explain to unbelievers that God had revealed the foundational cause of the unknown illness to me? The illness had kept us for over three months in the hospital without diagnosis or cure, and it was the best children's hospital in Germany. No wonder the Bible says God uses the foolish things of this world to confound the wise. It

GOD OF THE IMPOSSIBLE

was extremely difficult for me to persuade the doctors to even consider attempting my suggestion but, thankfully, God cannot lie.

Consequently, it got to a point where I wondered in my heart if it was God or my imagination. I added, If God intended to heal my daughter, why would He not just have her stop vomiting and get her system aligned so that we could be discharged? I questioned why God would tell me something that seemed so difficult for the physicians to attempt, putting us in even more danger. However, days went by, nothing changed, and no good progress could be made, but I kept the faith and believed that He would do it. Remember, God assured me that my daughter's circumstances would exalt His name.

As a result, I persisted and trusted in the God of the impossible.

CHAPTER 7

EL ROI THE GOD WHO SEES ME

Many of God's names in the Bible begin with "El," which refers to God. "Roi" (pronounced "ro-ee") is the Hebrew word for "see" or "look."

El-Roi was first mentioned in Genesis 16:1-13, where Hagar, a runaway and a poor servant, received God's promise in her hour of greatest need. She approached her predicament with a positive attitude and embraced God's offer of assistance for herself and her unborn child. It all started when Abram's wife, Sarai, offered to help Abram start their family. This was not God's plan, but it was a common practice at the time. Abram agreed to the plan, and Hagar became pregnant. Hagar began to despise her mistress, and Sarai suffered as a result

EL ROI THE GOD WHO SEES ME

of Hagar's proud and arrogant attitude. Although the plan was entirely Sarai's idea, Sarai began to cruelly mistreat Hagar. So, Hagar fled into the desert, eventually stopping near a spring of water. I cannot imagine her state of mind as she was alone, pregnant, and without options. In the midst of her difficulties, an angel of the Lord appeared to Sarai's maid and asked her where she had come from and where she was going. When Hagar admitted her plight, the angel told her in Genesis 16:9 -11:

"Return to your mistress and submit to her. I will multiply your descendants so that they will be too numerous to count; you will have a son, whom you shall name Ishmael, for the Lord has heard of your misery".

"So, she gave this name to the Lord who spoke to her: 'You are the God who sees me,' for she said, 'I have now seen the One who sees me'. That is why the well was called Beer Lahai Roi, it is still there, between Kadesh and Bered". Hagar learned a valuable lesson that day as she rested at the desert spring. God was watching over her and had plans to bless her, which is the most intriguing part of the story. What He did for Hagar continues to be a source of comfort for us today. It is reassuring to know that El Roi sees us in our struggles and comes to us.

BACK FROM THE DEAD

Regrettably, I have heard people say, out of all the billions of people in this world, does God even know that you exist? Could He single you out as an individual, or are you just unknown in the mass of humanity? Know that God sees you! As an individual, you are known by Him! He knows the very number of hairs on your head, according to Matthew 10:30. Consider that your worth is greater than the many sparrows in the sky, according to Luke 12:7. Also, consider that He took an intimate interest in forming you, that you are "fearfully and wonderfully made; that all of His "works [that being you!] are wonderful," according to Psalm 139:13 -14. He loves us so much, that He sent His only Son, Jesus Christ, to die a horrific death for us and our sins, so that we could be forgiven and reconciled back to God because He wants a relationship with us according to John 3:16 and Romans 5:8. Consider that we are his "workmanship, created in Christ Jesus for good works, which God prepared beforehand, that we should walk in them", according to Ephesians 2:10. That is how much we are known by God. And not only does He know us, but He also knows our names.

One thing that struck me about this Bible paragraph was that every time Sarah or Abraham referenced Hagar, she was simply referred to as "my slave" or "your slave" (Genesis 16:2, 5, 6). This leads me to believe that she was nothing more than a tool to be utilized for their own selfish gain: to twist God's

EL ROI THE GOD WHO SEES ME

plan to create an heir. I can only imagine how disheartening that had to be for Hagar.

However, when God discovered Hagar by the well, the first thing He said was, "Hagar" (16:8). When no one else cared enough to be decent to Hagar, God did. We do not know if Hagar knew who God was until that point in the story, but God clearly knew who Hagar was. He did in fact know her name and used it to show her respect. We feel the same way. God recognises our names. He knows each and every "sheep" by name because they are His treasured offspring (John 10:3). Our names are not only known to Him but they are "engraved" on the palm of His hand (Isaiah 49:16). Being etched has a more profound meaning than being written. It is "cut and carved" into God's palm, signifying permanence, something that cannot be erased.

El Roi is not blind to our struggle; our position has not surprised Him, as it may have surprised us, just as my daughter's case surprised me. He observes everything that happens to us every second of the day, good and evil, since He is omniscient (all-knowing). Our predicament, our very lives, are always in His sights. Nothing evades His heavenly observation or attention. I adore the fact that El Roi visited Hagar. He sought her out and arrived just as she needed Him. She needed to be comforted at that moment that she was seen that she was cherished and not forgotten, and that she and her unborn child (a boy whom God personally named; yet another special blessing God bestowed upon Hagar). God, as "the Father of compassion and the God of all comfort" (Psalm 147:3), calmed Hagar's fears and brought solace to her wounded, weary heart. God promises me, like He did to Hagar, that He will "never leave me nor forsake me" (Deuteronomy 31:6).

Similarly, El Roi bestows His love and mercy on me throughout my moments of greatest need. God sees you, dear friend, so rejoice! He understands what you are going through because, as Hagar put it, "you are [El Roi] a God of seeing". "Truly, I have seen Him who watches over me". (Genesis 16:13). Even the most vigilant parent must sleep, but the Bible makes it clear that God never sleeps, never looks one way while we look the other, and never misses a millisecond of what is happening on Earth. It also assures us that God is looking for men and women who are completely devoted to him. Why? Because he desires to fortify their hearts while they serve him. If you are feeling weak in the face of life's hardships, strengthening your devotion to Christ is the best way to grow stronger. Decide to obey Him entirely, to follow Him wholeheartedly, and to keep your gaze fixed on him. Allow El Roi to take joy in watching after you, and you will soon

EL ROI THE GOD WHO SEES ME

discover your heart stronger and your confidence deeper without realising it.

Since we serve a God who sees us, we are never alone. We may be at ease knowing that God is always aware of what we are going through. El Roi appeared to Hagar, but He did not guarantee a rapid solution to all of her difficulties. He sees us, but He also sees the bigger picture beyond the confines of time. God sometimes urges us to set limits and move away from abuse or mistreatment. In other cases, God wants us to persist with a new perspective in a challenging circumstance, be it marriage, work environment, or a church issue. We should consistently hold onto His promises. Have you ever been in a season of betrayal or struggle and wished for God to simply solve it? Have you ever felt like that? While El Roi sees our abuse, we must trust His guidance since He sees the overall picture. God knows when we cry buckets of tears for no apparent reason. He knows when we perfect a new skill or forgive a tough individual, and He rejoices with us. He notices us on bad days when all we feel is numbness. He may not immediately solve every problem we face, but we never have to doubt His existence. Because El Roi is the God who sees and makes sure we are never alone.

With this perspective, I continued to visit the hospital daily and to pray for victory. Even though no solution had emerged, I

BACK FROM THE DEAD

remained confident that God would carry out His promises. It was one of the most difficult times of my life, since going to the hospital was fraught with uncertainty. There was no evidence that God heard the prayers I made. Our God works in the background. "For this is what the LORD says: You will see neither wind nor rain, but this valley will be filled with water, and you, your cattle, and your other animals will drink," Elijah declares in 2 Kings 3:17. Sometimes we pray, and it appears that God is not listening to us, but He is. Please persevere, because if you do not doubt, you will undoubtedly see Him come through for you. This is exactly what happened to me; I continued to pray and fast as a small sacrifice, refusing to give up or doubt until He came through for us.

God notices us. He knows our names and loves us. We are His offspring, not just one among many. One thing is certain: nothing I go through is beyond His knowledge and comprehension because His Word is already ahead of the challenge. God was aware of the conflict I went through. I knew He understood what I required and that He would make provision. I recognised that it may not have been how I wanted it, but it would always be what was best for me. He has vowed to provide me with the strength, peace, and everything else I require each day. His authority is absolute. His grace is abundant, and His love is unfailing. We often take simple favours for granted. The fact that we are breathing, that our

EL ROI THE GOD WHO SEES ME

organs are working properly, and that most of us have food and water today should not be taken for granted. These are all gifts. If we sincerely look around, we can recognise God's everyday blessings. God is not always required to move mountains. He can provide shelter, food, and a loving family. We must keep track of all the ways in which He provides for us. In our most desperate moments, like Hagar, we may see God's fingerprints all over our past. We know He has the key to the future. And He will never stop looking after us.

I had reflected with deep appreciation on the previous weeks, months, and years, and I saw God act in incredible ways. I knew He had seen me through when no one else had. I have complete faith that He will continue to care for me even when I am in the deepest valley. So, a few days after the revelation from the Holy Spirit, the intravenous line spontaneously ruptured. Wow, I felt it was a big opportunity for me to be given a chance. So, I begged the medical practitioners not to fix it, but no one listened, and it was reconnected that evening. That night I cried and begged God to do the miraculous if He had actually spoken to me about the root cause of our lengthy hospital stay. Meanwhile, the doctors unceasingly searched for a cure for the mysterious ailment.

The paediatricians convened multidisciplinary meetings and discussed what could be done. A series of tests were carried

BACK FROM THE DEAD

out, many of which were quite painful for my daughter and me. We had to push her bed from department to department to perform these examinations. Undesirably, my daughter's continued hospitalisation made us quite popular at the hospital as people came and left, and we became the longest-staying patient-carer duo in her ward. Days passed by, and all I could think about was God performing the amazing. In all the battles, I reminded God that He was my rock and stronghold. We found healing and peace in Him, and I prayed for my child's healing.

As the Doctor of all doctors, I respectfully requested that He return her to full health. That He give her the strength and courage she needed to conquer her illness. She was too little to comprehend what she was going through. I beseeched God to please hold her hand and strengthen her spirit". I reminded God that one of the greatest joys for parents is to see their children grow healthy and robust. I implored Him to assist me in regaining my joy in seeing my child healthy and robust. I asked God to speak His healing and restoration Word into my child. I prayed to Him to give our family the strength to keep going through the difficult time. I asked Him to rekindle the fire in me so that I could continue to be committed and loyal to Him and His grace. I pleaded with Him to heal my child and restore her health.

CHAPTER 8

OUR AFFLICTIONS ARE TRANSIENT

God promises not only to replace our sorrow with pleasure but also to transform it into joy. Jesus said, "I tell you the truth, you will grieve and mourn while the rest of the world rejoices; you will grieve, but you will ultimately experience pleasure. A woman in labour experiences pain because her time has come, but when her child is born, she forgets the agony due to her elation at the birth of a child". (John 16:20 -22). It could also be rendered as "your grief will become joy". According to The Message Bible, "you will be sad, very sad, but your sadness will transform into joy". Similarly, sorrow becomes pleasure in Esther 9:22, sobbing becomes dancing in Psalm 30:11, and anguish becomes joy in Jeremiah 31:13.

OUR AFFLICTIONS ARE TRANSIENT

A lady who is about to give birth feels pain that is closely tied to her imminent happiness. The infant is born from pain, and thus the joy of having a child is born from pain. God transforms sorrow into joy. Suffering is both eclipsed and redeemed by happiness. I have recognised that, much like soldiers resuming their lives after returning from war, how we respond to tragedy impacts the fate of events. In reality, the nature of the tragedy is unimportant in the final analysis. King David wrote: "Weeping may last for the night, but a shout of joy comes in the morning". We have all undoubtedly experienced mourning following a loss of some kind, whether it is the loss of a job, money, opportunity, or the inability to maintain close relationships with families and colleagues. Grief is not intended to destroy us; rather, it is intended to transform us. Grief is not a form of punishment but a part of life.

Although Jesus is our greatest joy, we must not overlook emotional pain. As God's children, we should be developing our belief that He alone is the source of our lasting fulfilment, satisfaction, and joy. However, addressing our emotional suffering is crucial. Life is a difficult endeavour. As Christians, we do not believe that nothing bad will happen to us. Jesus did not promise that no weapon would be fashioned against us, but He did promise that no weapon fashioned against us would be effective (Isaiah 54:17). As a result, we learn what it is like to "walk through the valley of the shadow of death" and

BACK FROM THE DEAD

live "in the presence of our enemies" (Psalm 23:4 - 6). The good news is that we are fighting from the point of victory, and the Bible tells us that when the enemy comes in like a flood, God's spirit will raise a banner against him" (Isaiah 59:19). When we face misfortune, we should not ask, "Why me?" since God knows our capabilities and will not give us more than we can handle. It is time to work together with the Holy Spirit on a combat strategy. There will always be times of agony and loss in the lives of both believers and nonbelievers; the difference is how we respond to them.

I have found myself on the battlefield on countless occasions. It can be quite distressing and heartbreaking at times, but the outcome decides the conflict. Battles have become an integral part of my life, and I see them as stepping stones to the next level. My daughter's situation was one of them. I recall that the first time I was confronted with life's harsh reality was when I was a young teenager. I was thirteen or fourteen years old. My family adopted a German Shepherd named Buky, a fantastic dog in many ways, and I liked him. However, he had several physical impairments, making it difficult for us to meet his needs. I will never forget the night he died; I truly saw him battle for his life to the end. That evening, I sobbed myself to sleep. Similar emotions have resurfaced repeatedly during my life, including, my daughter's prolonged hospitalisation, death and return to life.

OUR AFFLICTIONS ARE TRANSIENT

Maybe the same is true for you as it was for Jesus' disciples. As a dedicated shepherd and guide, Jesus tried to prepare His disciples for life's difficult challenges. They wanted earthly rule and an end to the injustices of their time, but He gave them a cross instead. Despite their inability to understand at first, He taught them regardless, instilling in them the truth they needed for a balanced outlook on life. Believing the truth about Jesus gives me victory in all situations. Also, the truth concerning Jesus enables me to approach these truths with an optimistic and hopeful perspective that is unparalleled by any other viewpoint.

Jesus clarifies this by declaring that we shall suffer both emotional and physical suffering in this world. As Christians, we occasionally indulge in self-pity, thinking we are not meant to suffer. When Jesus spoke to His disciples about the hard truths of life, He addressed issues that are universal to all people, from birth to death. Both believers and non-believers suffer the consequences of sin and the agony of death. When Jesus discussed these challenges with His followers, He also mentioned the hardships that those who follow Him will endure. In addition to the typical trials of life, believers have additional challenges (John 16:33). However, we will rejoice in the end.

It is the truth that believers will suffer both emotionally and physically in this world. This is an unavoidable fact of life. We are not permitted to go over or beneath the barrier. We must persevere, but God promises never to abandon nor forsake us. Being unsure about Jesus puts one at a disadvantage. Even though there is no way in this world to avoid pain and suffering, there is a way to go through it with purpose and emerge victorious. To do so, we must first comprehend Jesus' teachings. What impact does His teaching have on how we respond to difficult and negative life experiences? Is our response to adversity and suffering "run and hide" strategy and "be afraid and depressed" feelings? Or is it more like the "run to Scripture" approach?

Believing the truth about Jesus will enable us to triumph in all spheres of life. Jesus asked His followers an important question. "Do you now believe?" (John 16:31). He added, "A time is coming and in fact has come when you will be scattered, each to your own home. You will leave me all alone. Yet I am not alone, for my Father is with me". It is important to react in faith after hearing and comprehending the truth about Jesus. Faith is letting go of the many erroneous beliefs we cling to, for stability and significance with the fingers of our heart and brain. In the world, some believe that they are not sinners at all, while others believe they can mend their broken relationship with God, by traditional methods, religious activities, moral behaviour, and charitable gestures. Conversely, some believe that God and eternity are only

OUR AFFLICTIONS ARE TRANSIENT

myths, and that God does not exist. These beliefs do not give their followers joy. It is only in Christianity that a person finds joy because joy is a uniquely Christian feeling; it is a kind of happiness and gladness that a Christian can have that a nonbeliever cannot. The joy that Jesus offers is unique because of the circumstances that allow it. What exactly are these conditions? The death and resurrection of Jesus. When you accept Jesus as your Lord and Saviour, His death and resurrection benefit you personally. You are no longer guilty since Jesus died in your place for your sin. You have an eternally victorious connection with God because of His resurrection from the grave.

Jesus' resurrection represents a permanent and conclusive victory over all evil (John 16:33); it also allows for the most lasting happiness. Christian joy is predicated on events, specifically Christ's death and resurrection. It also provides for the most lasting joy because the resurrection of Jesus marks a permanent and conclusive victory over all evil (John 16:33). We must ponder on Jesus' death and resurrection as Christians. For this reason, it is critical to observe the Lord's Supper.

To return to my testimony: while my baby remained in the hospital, her intravenous feeding line broke for the second time in the afternoon of that day, and something extraordinary happened. As the physicians did not instantly refix it, God revealed to me that my daughter had eaten without vomiting. I attempted again to persuade them to delay the reinstallation of the feeding catheter until the following day, but no one listened. I kept thinking about what I could do until one fateful day, God turned my grief into gladness as the feeding catheter ruptured for the third time. I hoped that the doctor would not find a vein to replace it. I begged God not to allow the doctor to fix the damaged catheter. I prayed and said that if God had given me this revelation, He should please prove Himself.

That evening, the doctor worked for hours trying to find a vein. Finally, the doctor suggested that he would take my daughter to the surgery as soon as possible. That was the beginning of my victory. I told the right nurse straightaway that I did not want the doctors to fix it again. So, the nursed advised that I could object to it, but I would have to sign for it. That evening, I told my husband everything and urged him to please stand by me in the matter. He was sceptical at first because he could not see how a feeding tube could cause vomiting. I begged him to believe me because God had revealed it to me, and he consented.

Thankfully, I had already informed the night nurse of my opposition to the replacement of the intravenous feeding tube. That night, I could not sleep as I checked into my hotel.

OUR AFFLICTIONS ARE TRANSIENT

Thoughts raced through my head: "What if it is not God and it is just my imagination?" and "What if something terrible happens to my daughter as a result of my decision"? However, I disregarded all the thoughts and clung to the Holy Spirit. The next morning, I arrived at the hospital at 5 a.m. and the doctors arrived at 6 a.m. When the doctors came, they held a multidisciplinary discussion with all of my daughter's medical professionals. In the conference, they highlighted all the consequences of what I was about to do, including going to prison if something bad occurred to my baby, because of my failure to provide medical care. I agreed and signed all the documents before my baby was entrusted in my care. Though I was fearful, the Holy Spirit helped me to forge ahead.

A few hours later, after I had signed all the documents, my baby cried excessively, and I became anxious since I could not figure out what the issue was. I requested a bottle of baby milk, which I fed her with. I was not sure if she had missed the meal from the feeding catheter or if there had been a detrimental impact on the removal. So, I continued and fed her but shockingly, for the first time in nearly four months, my baby did not vomit after she was fed. It felt like a dream! After two hours she sobbed again, and they brought her more infant formula, which she consumed without vomiting. My heart began to rejoice, and I realised it had to be God. The feeding continued throughout the day, and every time the doctors and

BACK FROM THE DEAD

nurses checked to see if she was deteriorating so they could charge me but, to their amazement, the report was always positive.

CHAPTER 9

BYE HOSPITAL. WELCOME HOME

The following day, when my baby's medical practitioners checked on her, they were all astonished and confused by the development she had made. They were astounded to see that in addition to eating, my child had gained weight and was more interactive. Remember that by this time she had already spent nearly four months in the hospital. So, on the third day, the doctors decided that we did not need to be in the hospital any longer because my baby had significantly improved, she had been eating and drinking normally, and she had been consistently gaining weight. Considering the ongoing progress, a discharge planning meeting was held, and the doctors conveyed their deep regret to my family.

BACK FROM THE DEAD

They stated that they regretted not listening to me earlier. They asked if there was any way they could make up for all the time spent in the hospital, and they acknowledged that in all their years of experience, it had never occurred to them that an intravenous tube could cause a child's illness. They explained that the intravenous tube has always been a source of nourishment for sick people who are unable to eat and drink conventionally. They said they had never been any problems with it; and that without intravenous feeding, the patient's condition would deteriorate, and it could lead to their death if they lack the essential nutrients to fight illness and disease.

They added that it was unclear to them if the problem was because of the child's African heritage but, they acknowledged that they had treated numerous African children without encountering such an issue. Shockingly, they conceded that their profession was thrown into disarray when a non-medical professional provided a cure for a disease that they had been unable to diagnose for months. Nonetheless, they thanked me so much for standing my ground and approaching them with such courage and assurance. They went on and on with their explanations and bewilderment. In the end, they concluded that we would be discharged the following day, which was the third day my baby had eaten without vomiting. I thanked them for the opportunity, though it was delayed, and I was glad that at least I was given one. I made it clear to them that I am a believer who receives

GOODBYE HOSPITAL. WELCOME HOME

revelations and instructions from the Holy Spirit.

Unfortunately, they did not share my point of view on this and instead made medical excuses for what had occurred. Fortunately, the doctor who had delivered the devastating news to me after my child was certified dead, remarked how startled she was. She recalled me saying 'My child will not die', and the child did not die! She explained that from a medical standpoint, they had determined that she would not survive, but that everything had miraculously reversed, and appeared so incredible to them.

The meeting that day was full of regrets and reflections, but the most exciting news was that we were leaving the hospital the next day as there was no longer any need to keep us. After four months in the hospital, I felt so relieved when the day finally arrived. I could not wait to get home and sleep in my bed, surrounded by familiar faces and surroundings. Yes, my daughter had miraculously come back from the brink of death. She was nothing short of miraculous, and God had once again proved His dominion over the very core of existence. It is not over unless He says so.

Then, I remembered that I had not eaten breakfast in four months and had not missed my midnight warfare. I recalled a time when it appeared as if God was not interested in all my spiritual sacrifices. However, God was working behind the scenes.

Looking back, I imagine that despite my knowledge of God's Word, I still require practical application of the Word for it to function. Although having a basic understanding of God's Word is a foundational step, it may be ineffective unless we put it into practice. Even if God has provided us with a life road map, it is still necessary that we act and put the Word into practice for it to be effective in our daily existence. Food has been provided by God; it is our responsibility to consume it. As it is expected of us to participate in life's events, God will not place food in our mouths if we refuse to consume it when it is provided. Thus, we are equipped with everything necessary to navigate life.

In addition, a man of God from Uganda, Joshua Kawalya, states in his book *Delivered from Deep Darkness* that confession, conviction, and contention are necessary when fighting a battle. This means that in times of disaster, we must consistently declare, believe, and wage war with God's Word. My little experience has shown me that the devil is fighting us with spiritual laziness, since he knows that when we pray, things will get better. So, he does everything to stop us from praying as he knows that if we comprehend the things of the Spirit, we will come up with plans and techniques that will enable us to rise above spiritual slothfulness and resume our prayer life when he attacks our prayers.

God declares that nothing will harm us and that we can trample over snakes and scorpions and all of the enemy's capabilities (Luke 10:19). Equally, according to Luke 11:21-22, "When a strong man with weapons guards his palace, his goods are in peace", but "when a stronger man shall come upon him and overcome him, he takes from him all his armour in which he trusted and divides his spoils". As God's children, we can conquer all obstacles and enter the enemy's camp to seize what is rightfully ours. The Bible is quite explicit in saying that we have all we need to win this war. Keep in mind that the Holy Spirit is our fighter and that we are not alone in this struggle since we are fighting from a position of triumph.

Notably, we achieve what we fight for in life, not what we wish for. Remember, we cannot eat if we do not work. When we decide to fight, the Holy Spirit provides us with the knowledge of how to do so, and the means to do so are already available Ephesians 6:13-18 says, "Put on all of God's armour, then, so that you can hold your ground and stand when the day of evil arrives and after you've done everything you can. Now stand firmly, with the breastplate of righteousness in place, the gospel of peace fitting into your feet, and the belt of truth wrapped around your waist. Take up the shield of faith in addition to all of this, so that you can stop the evil one's fiery arrows. Accept the sword of the Spirit, God's Word, and the helmet of salvation. And make all types of petitions and prayers in the Spirit at all times. Keep this in mind as you remain vigilant and continue to pray for all of the people of the Lord". With this information, success is guaranteed.

I also understood that consistency in all we do is crucial in spiritual battles, as there is a pattern to break. The Bible teaches us consistency through the parable of the widow and the unjust judge in Luke 18:1-8. The biblical account of the widow and the judge was one of the sources from which I drew inspiration for this lengthy battle. The narrative placed a lot of emphasis on perseverance. The widow did not give up until the judge grew tired of her pleading and resolved to act on her behalf. Each night, following my conflict with the adversary, I would turn to God and tell Him that I had come as a widow. He is the judge, and I was the widow who refused to give up until He avenged for me. I would let Him know that I would not rest until my supplication was granted.

Thankfully, I am happy that God had mercy on my little sacrifices, my desperation, and my unwillingness to give up. It was a lengthy and solitary war that ended in praise with the Holy Spirit at the forefront. Every battle calls for perseverance, commitment, and faith in God. Without this determination, defeat is inevitable. Remember, if you are a Christian, that the adversary is searching for people to devour. Have this approach and be determined that he will not get you or your family.

The widow's narrative revolves around consistency. Recall that during the entire ordeal, I fasted and waged war every midnight for the entire four months. I made up my mind to keep doing this till the devil took his hideous hand off my daughter. Though this is not a template for spiritual warfare it is how I felt at the time. The Holy Spirit is with us to provide direction and assistance in all the challenges of life. I included some of the spiritual sacrifices that I made in the story because people's stories can occasionally inspire others to take certain actions on their spiritual journey.

All in all, remember that God works in different ways, and always pray in the Spirit. Ephesians 6:18 encourages us to pray always in the spirit, with perseverance, making our supplication known to God. Also, Jude 1:20 encourages us to build up ourselves on our most holy faith, by praying in the Holy Ghost. For its part, Romans 8:26-27 states that "likewise the Spirit also helps our infirmities: for we know not what we should pray for as we ought: but the Spirit itself makes intercession for us with groanings which cannot be uttered. And he that searches the hearts knows the mind of the Spirit,

BACK FROM THE DEAD

because he makes intercession for the saints according to the will of God."

Furthermore, Joshua Kawalya, explained in his book that when we pray in the Spirit, we are sending out signals. God can raise people who pick up the prayer in the spirit and intercede for us through the Spirit. Therefore, it is crucial that we pray in the Spirit, continue to be steadfast, remain consistent, and never yield to the enemy. Keep in mind that according to God's Word, everything that is hurled at us on the battlefield is working for our good. Remember to approach every battle with the warrior mentality. Do not forget that sometimes, it is possible to sustain injuries on the battlefield. In that case, don't display a self-pity mentality; rather, refuel with God's Word, and rejoin the fight knowing that you will undoubtedly prevail through the help of the Holy Spirit.

That night, after the discharge planning meeting at the hospital, I reflected about the entire process on the battlefield. I had no choice but to praise the Holy Spirit who fought the whole battle. I chuckled and added, "Now that the battle is over, I can eat and sleep peacefully". That evening, I celebrated Thanksgiving in my hotel room. I thanked the Holy Spirit for reassurance when I could neither see the wind nor the rain, but He made me remain steadfast and consistent and sustained my belief that the battle was already won.

GOODBYE HOSPITAL. WELCOME HOME

The devil is aware that he is a loser, but he will continue to fight. He will avoid us if we pay attention to God's Word and allow it to bear fruit in our hearts to the point where it becomes our weapon. My advice to anyone reading this book is to never give up when confronted with an unpleasant circumstance. God is called El Roi. The God who sees you will come to your aid. He has not forgotten you, and He will not forget you, just as He did not forget Haggar. If you are born again, you are worth considerably more than Haggar since He purchased you through the blood of Jesus Christ.

Therefore, you are so important to Him that He will never forget you. Please, continue to trust, believe, and persevere because He sees you and will undoubtedly provide for you. However, if you are not born again, you can do so now because the Holy Spirit only works with those who have accepted Jesus as their Lord and personal Saviour. The Holy Spirit is the doing arm of God. When the resurrected Jesus was leaving the earth, He promised believers that He would send them the Holy Spirit who would teach them all things (John 14:26). Many have also testified that you can never have genuine peace of mind or eternity until you surrender to Jesus Christ. All you need is to confess that Jesus is Lord with your mouth and believe in your heart that God raised Him from the dead (Romans 10:9). Then you will be saved, and the Holy Spirit will reside in your heart and teach you all things.

BACK FROM THE DEAD

Back to the testimony. That day, after our hospital discharge planning meeting, I somehow felt both thrilled and frightened as I prepared for my baby to return home,. I became concerned about how I would care for my baby at home without the usual support I had been receiving. These emotions are normal, and many parents experience them after a long stay in the hospital. As the professionals on the ward assisted us in preparing for discharge, the staff was confident in my ability to care for her which reassured me. We held a small celebration and took photographs as mementos. Suddenly, the professionals in the unit became grieved by our leaving. After four months together, we had become like a family. Other families whose children were hospitalised in the ward also had conflicted emotions because we were the oldest family on the ward. Families arrived and left us there, but fortunately, we had preached hope and encouragement to them and even brought some to Christ.

Finally, the doctors handed us a discharge statement, and the letter stated that things could change depending on a variety of factors, including my baby's health and stability, my skill and confidence to manage her at home, the level of support at home, and the availability of follow-up care. They also explained that my daughter would not be a normal child again because she had been on medication for a very long time. They also posited that because she had been fed through an

GOODBYE HOSPITAL. WELCOME HOME

intravenous tube for a long time, it would be difficult for her to eat solid food when required and that she would not be able to walk for at least two years or more. They added that everything about her would be delayed and abnormal, but I should not be concerned because this was due to what she had passed through. After listening to their medical report, I dropped my baby at the hospital entrance and made my own declarations. I stated that I gave them the old child and carried the new child out of the hospital. I declared that this new child would speak when her siblings spoke, and she would walk when her siblings walked. She would consume the same food as her siblings. I announced that I had abandoned the previous child, who was riddled with complications and abnormalities, in favour of a new child who would reach all developmental milestones, and I returned home with the new child.

However, I came home from the hospital that day feeling odd. Some medical partitioners fail to address what happens to patients after they are discharged from the hospital following a protracted stay. I believe that some hospitals fail to recognise that some families may require emotional and psychological support, as part of their loved one's recovery plan, to reduce deterioration or emotional breakdown. It also goes to reason that the more serious a person's medical condition, the more crucial the hospital-to-home transition is required. Researchers have discovered that two-thirds of critically ill patients who require an intensive care unit (ICU) stay are experiencing physical, psychological, or social problems. They recommend that ICU personnel and other professionals educate patients and their families about the likelihood of needing various types of help for months after being discharged from the ICU or a lengthy hospital stay. Fortunately, Jesus is my emotional and psychological stability.

Honestly, the support is extremely essential because it will relieve parents of a great deal of mental and psychological stress especially for some who may struggle. Initially, providing home care for my baby proved to be somewhat difficult due to her prolonged hospitalisation. My daughter and I had not built a personal bond because she had been under the care of multiple professionals. Breastfeeding was challenging because she had never been breastfed before, and the hospital primarily used extraction. Her inability to be breastfed and other peculiar behaviours gave me several restless nights. However, when I remembered the doctor's entire report, I declared that she was a new person, with the doctor's report behind her. I trusted the Holy Spirit's work on her. I never awoke at night to feed my other children. However, because she was unfamiliar with lactation, my daughter declined the offer to breastfeed at night. I would rise in the middle of the night to prepare baby formula or extract

GOODBYE HOSPITAL. WELCOME HOME

breast milk for her, but by the time I finished, she would have fallen asleep. She could not be roused by any amount of prodding, and whenever I fell asleep, she woke up again. Due to the family dynamics at the time, I was unable to sleep during the day. God did not make a mistake when He created the night for sleep, and it can become difficult for some people to sleep during the day if they miss their night-time sleep. At the time, I could only sleep during the day if everything was quiet, but this was not the case. We eventually received assistance, as I had neither family nor friends available to provide support. After a few months, everything blossomed, she began to breastfeed, and we formed a strong bond.

Regarding her developmental achievement, it was as if nothing had ever occurred to her. At her six-month check-up, the physicians and nurses on duty were astonished by her progress. They stated that she had disproved them and that everything about her contradicted their medical profession. What they did not comprehend was that the Holy Spirit was in command, not them. I believe the biblical passage, which states that God employs the foolish things of the world to confound the wise (1 Corinthians 1:27).

My understanding of life is that there are both facts and truths. Fact can be defined as head knowledge - items acquired through learning, experience, and research, but fact is surpassed by the truth. The truth is God's Word. According to the Bible, if we comprehend this truth, it will set us free; the truth is the Word of God that we hold over our circumstances. If we believe it, the written Word will set us free. We can accomplish this through confession, proclamation, and faith. The Bible states that God's Word will not return to Him void; it must accomplish His will and reach its intended recipient (Isaiah 55:11). This means that if you capture the rhema, the Word becomes yours at that moment, and if you hold onto it, there will be a performance.

Some of us face the challenge of devoting time to persevere in God's presence. Most Christians anticipate a fast fix from God, and when this is not the case, weariness sets in. We must learn how to linger in God's presence. We are so occupied that it is difficult for us to dwell in His presence. My prayer is that, despite the busyness of our lives, God will help us discern how to tarry and persevere because there are battles that can drag on and will require determination and perseverance from us. When God sees that we are unwilling to give up and cling to the truth of His Word, He will grant us success. God will bring His Word to pass by manifesting it.

As Christians, we must always be prepared for war, as we are all soldiers of Christ.

To clarify my analogy between fact and truth, a fact remains a

GOODBYE HOSPITAL. WELCOME HOME

fact until it is refuted by the truth. This indicates that physicians' medical terminologies are accurate until they are overruled by the truth, which is referred to as God's Word. How do I know? Permit me to share this brief anecdote that strengthened my conviction in what I am saying.

When we returned home, my daughter walked in less than a year and consumed solid foods immediately. It appeared as if we had never visited the hospital. I knew it was God in action, but the devil told me that it was just a coincidence. Good thing I was fortunate to have the number of one of the parents I preached to in the ward. The Holy Spirit prompted me to contact her. Unfortunately, her daughter and my daughter had experienced similar health challenges, and they were discharged before us because she was a medical professional and could care for her daughter at home. Therefore, she was permitted to transport everything necessary to care for her daughter at home from the hospital. So, I contacted her when our children were 18 months old. She reported that her child was unable to consume solid foods and was receiving intravenous feeding and occasional small amounts of milk. She could not even crawl, let alone walk. Everything the doctor stated regarding her child played out, and I prayed with her. When my daughter was three years old, I contacted her again. The story had not changed; her daughter was still unable to walk and unable to eat solid foods.

BACK FROM THE DEAD

I ultimately lost contact with her and have no idea what happened after that.

I began to ponder how advantageous it is for us to be God's children and how we can declare things and have them stand. Our God is concerned about us. Although I had encouraged the lady, I was unable to convince her to engage in warfare prayers with me because she was a new convert and did not understand the things of the Spirit. In addition, language was a significant barrier for me because most of the information I wished to share was best conveyed in English and not German. Though I was very disappointed that I could not do much due to my limitations, I prayed that God would reverse her daughter's condition just like mine. The story of my daughter's miraculous recovery from the claws of death continues to shame the devil because if I had believed everything the physicians told me, everything would have played out. The Bible states that whatever we bind on earth is bound in Heaven and whatever we lose on earth is also losed in Heaven (Mathew 18:18). This demonstrates that whenever we are given a negative report, we should instantly reject it. Everything we agree upon is accepted and everything we reject is rejected. I pray that God will grant us all the understanding and wisdom to complete this race. In the name of Jesus!

CHAPTER 10

HOSPITAL EVANGELISM IS BORN

This account of how God brought my daughter back to life is evidence that life is full of both good and bad surprises. Positive experiences are wonderful. However, negative occurrences or circumstances are more likely to help a person mature and appreciate the complexities of life. Such experiences, when properly evaluated, can provide new understanding, comprehension, faith, and appreciation of God. Her story demonstrates how establishing a relationship with God can truly change a person's life and circumstances. A reader of this book will probably be able to identify with many of the doubts, anxieties, and obstacles that we faced during the journey. Similarly, throughout our lives, we will come across friends and families who are in pain and suffering that we can encourage. This was how I found faith amid adversity. I believe that our story will in some way inspire others.

Following everything we went through. The Holy Spirit revealed to me how I could help other children and their parents by visiting hospitals, supporting parents, praying for children, and giving small presents. I started my experience in Nigeria by donating items to orphans. I also ship things from the United Kingdom to Nigeria to orphanages. I visit intensive care units in the UK, where I live, to inform families about my experience and offer prayers. God has been extremely wonderful in this regard. Now and again, I take these children's names and continue to pray for them. As a result, others learn about Jesus Christ's gospel. In Luke 22:32, Jesus tells Peter, "But I have prayed for you, Simon, that your faith may not fail. And when you have turned back, strengthen your brothers". Since God has saved me, I must, in some little way, strengthen others.

Christians use the term 'testimony' to describe recounting a story to demonstrate what Christ has done in their lives. Thus, a witness is merely recounting Christ's work in their life. A witness is a composite of three narratives: God's story, your

HOSPITAL EVANGELISM IS BORN

story, and the people with whom you are sharing it. For example, the vast story of what God is doing in the world, your personal account of how God has transformed your life, and a call to action, asking, "How would this impact their lives"? In the Bible, people such as the apostle Paul have frequently recounted their own testimonies. An example is the conversion of Saul on the road to Damascus, detailed in Acts 9:1-12. I do believe that sharing my personal story is an effective evangelism technique. People are interested in hearing about your encounter with God and how He has transformed your life. Your story may not be like mine, but we all have unique stories of what God has done, and we must share them so that Jesus will be glorified, and others can learn about God's faithfulness.

Being a witness is so compelling because, regardless of your philosophical position, you cannot deny a change, or even a miracle, in the life of another person. The man born blind in the ninth chapter of John exclaimed, "I was blind, but now I can see because of Jesus". And they wished for him to be excluded from the synagogue. It is so dramatic because the change is unquestionable. A testimony is an opportunity to ask someone, "What do you think of this change, regardless of where you stand"? People like to listen to testimonies because we live in a culture that is so fond of storytelling. On multiple occasions, when I shared my story, individuals remarked, "You almost convinced me to believe". Similar to what the Bible says about Agrippa in Acts 26:28, the Apostle Paul nearly persuaded him.

We must strive to make our stories more about God than about ourselves while remaining personal and relatable. I appreciate hearing the stories of others. It is essential that we share the spiritual steps we have taken so that others can learn from them. Sometimes it may not have been these steps that led to victory; other times, God may have shown mercy because of the spiritual steps. Some individuals, however, do not believe in sharing their testimony with others because they believe it steals the spotlight away from God. Remember how, after healing the ten lepers, Jesus instructed them to report to the priest. In other words, go and testify. Testimonies are an essential component of evangelism. I recall recently testifying in church and a church member coming to meet with me to express how my testimony had benefited her. This could be because she experienced a similar situation to which I testified or because her hopes were granted. I give thanks to God for the Holy Spirit, who prompted me to testify on that day.

God may sometimes want us to share things that would bring glory to His name, but if we are not spiritually sensitive, we may neglect Him, and the person who was to be blessed on

HOSPITAL EVANGELISM IS BORN

that day will be deprived. I believe that God has rescued us for us to save others; we have endured what we have endured so that others will not face the same difficulty. Experience sharing is indispensable.

Sharing our testimonies with others after achieving victory does not constitute self-glorification; it is a form of evangelism, as God's spirit provides direction. It is up to individuals to learn from the Holy Spirit how to pass through their suffering. I pray that God will give us wisdom and understanding for His work in Jesus' name. Probably, the widow in Luke 18 would not have received her miracle had she not persisted. In times of difficulty, we must take some spiritual measures since we have nothing to lose whether they work or fail. It is even more advantageous for us because it will strengthen our faith. If fasting does not produce spiritual fruit, Jesus will not say that this type can be eliminated only through fasting and prayer. (Matthew 17:21). God is merciful and will always show pity for our small sacrifices.

Likewise, a relationship with Christ instils a natural desire to share one's faith. A person in love regularly thinks about and discusses the object of their adoration. A person who has experienced Jesus Christ has a comparable longing. Acts 4:20 says, "it is impossible for us not to speak about what we have seen and heard". There is no better beginning point than to be used as a tool. Evangelism is fundamentally a divine activity; God is already at work in the lives of others and wants to use us to reach out to them. God prefers to operate through us rather than around us. God has put us in a special position at a special time to talk about Him. He wants us to represent Him wherever we go, be at work, at home, and everywhere else.

During evangelism, we encounter a variety of people, some of whom are not Christians because they have never heard of God. For this reason, it is sometimes beneficial to share testimonies so that they can imagine what life with God is like. Having spent a significant amount of time in the hospital, particularly in the intensive care unit (ICU), I believe it would be beneficial to share my story with other families going through similar difficulties. Whenever I share my encounter in the hospital, particularly in ICUs, on how God helped me surmount adversity, they are often interested and want to know more. The majority agree when I ask if I may pray for them and their hospitalised children. Occasionally, my daughter accompanies me as evidence, and people will continue to stare at her in the hope that one day they too will have a story to tell.

I only do what I am instructed to do, as only God can truly alter a person's heart. However, I can convey the individual's need

HOSPITAL EVANGELISM IS BORN

to the Holy Spirit, who will then work through the individual. I believe God wants to use us to make a difference with the people He wants us to speak to. We have seen Him at work most of the time, and I am aware that we are a part of what God is doing. God is also concerned with those in our lives who are not yet His followers.

As individuals, we are inherently connected to certain people in our lives due to our shared passions. Perhaps, our children may attend the same school, or we may originate from the same area. It is therefore natural for us to wish to discuss our values, including our faith in God, with these individuals. Equally, God desires a connection with them, on our own. We can simply ask God how He intends to use us in the spiritual journey of others. Daily prayers for the intervention of God in the lives of others can also strengthen our faith. God may use anything or anyone to disseminate His message. However, He desires to utilise us as we continue to pursue new opportunities for spiritual advancement. Before Jesus ascended into heaven, He told His disciples, "Surely I am with you always, to the very end of the age". Matthew 28:20 says He is always with us and will never abandon us. Whatever He instructs us to do, we can have confidence that He will be with us.

BACK FROM THE DEAD

I believe this narrative would be incomplete without gratitude to God. I say thank you Jesus for everything He has done and continues to do for me and my family. I want to express my deepest gratitude and reverence to God. It is due to God's mercy that I can share this testimony. I am grateful to God for providing my daughter with life when it seemed she had none. I praise God for His infallible Word, unconditional love, and unbreakable promises. God continues to perform miracles. Ultimately, He is a God who fulfils His promises. Also, I am eternally grateful to the staff members who extended assistance to me during that moment of profound sadness and anxiety. In addition, to the parent support group, where I interacted with other families experiencing similar circumstances, I say thank you.

As you conclude your reading of this book, I want to thank you for your patience. I do not know if you are facing any challenges in your life right now that seem intractable. I stand on the Word of God today as I stood during my daughter's affliction, and decree according to Job 22:28, that the matter is resolved speedily in the Name of Jesus! As you wait for that situation to pass away, I would like you to remember the great things that God has accomplished in your life. Give thanks for those things and believe that He will replicate the same victory in your life. Remember also that God's people in time's past

HOSPITAL EVANGELISM IS BORN

accomplished great feats in His Name and your story will be the same. Hebrews 10: 29-35 says:

"By faith [God's children] passed through the Red sea as by dry land: which the Egyptians assaying to do were drowned. By faith the walls of Jericho fell down, after they were compassed about seven days. By faith the harlot Rahab perished not with them that believed not when she had received the spies with peace. And what shall I more say? for the time would fail me to tell of Gedeon, and of Barak, and of Samson, and of Jephthae; of David also, and Samuel, and of the prophets: Who through faith subdued kingdoms, wrought righteousness, obtained promises, stopped the mouths of lions. Quenched the violence of fire, escaped the edge of the sword, out of weakness were made strong, waxed valiant in fight, turned to flight the armies of the aliens. Women received their dead raised to life again".

May our lives continue to be full of victories for we are more than conquerors!

ABOUT THE AUTHOR

Stella Ezekweh is a minister of God with a strong passion for the gospel of Jesus Christ. She is a leader with several leadership responsibilities. Stella's overarching desire is that all may come to God and experience the power of His might.

She is the founder and director of Zion Virtual Outreach, an organisation that visits hospitals to minister to parents and their sick children. Stella is very compassionate and empathetic towards parents who have sick children. Her passion for the well-being of children stems from her personal experience dealing with her child, who was proclaimed dead in the hospital after a protracted illness but miraculously came back to life.

Zion Virtual Outreach also supports motherless baby homes in Nigeria. Stella's passion to help others does not end there.

Stella is a social worker with MASH (Multi-Agency Safeguarding Hub). She is a Practice Educator and a Best Interest Assessor. She is a parenting practitioner with Advanced CCA. Stella also works with 'looked after children' and unaccompanied 16-18-year-old asylum seekers as an advisor.

She has strong business acumen, and she is currently

ABOUT THE AUTHOR

involved in real estate, but her passion is walking the halls of academia as she is an avid believer in the correlation between knowledge and service to mankind. She is a graduate of Mass Communication from one of Nigeria's premier universities, the University of Lagos. She also holds a master's in social work from Manchester University and is currently pursuing her doctorate at the same institution.

Stella is also a prolific author and publisher. She uses her writing to convey deep teachings to God's people. She is happily married to Sunny Nduka Ezekweh. By the grace of God, they both have six beautiful children, three boys and three girls.

BACK FROM THE DEAD

HAVE YOU FOUND YOUR PURPOSE YET?

Let Stella's Book Born For A Reason Guide You To Discover And Recover Your True Purpose On Earth.
AVAILABLE ON AMAZON

SCAN CODE TO PURCHASE

READERS NOTES

READERS NOTES

READERS NOTES